page 53

UNCUMBER
AND
PANTALOON

Gillian Edwards

UNCUMBER

AND

PANTALOON

SOME WORDS WITH STORIES

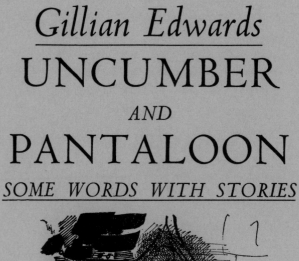

Illustrated by John Ward

E. P. DUTTON & CO., INC

To the Ratepayers of
Cambridge
in Gratitude for the
Books I Consulted
and the
Library where I worked

FOREWORD

This book was conceived when I idly wondered one day about the origin of the word *pants*, and traced it right back to a Greek saint, Pantaleone. There must, I thought, be other words that once, in an age when religion interlocked with life at every level, had their roots in the teaching, practice, tradition or legends of the Church, and have now lost that connexion. When I looked for them I found far more than I could cram into one book.

It is intended for those who enjoy collecting useless information, and is full of tales that have little foundation in fact. History, and especially the history of language, is shaped not by the truth but by what most people believe to be the truth. And among the people, as Father Thurston has said, "the senses predominate over the intelligence . . . Hence it is that popular legends overflow with marvels. Visions, prophecies and miracles play a necessary part in the lives of the saints." It is often these legends that have given our words their present form and colour, and the history of their meaning is the history of ourselves.

Moreover I have often been enticed from my main course to follow other words down other by-ways. For this I apologise but am unrepentant. "The heart," says Giacomo Leopardi, in Iris Origo's translation, "at last tires of all things; of sleep, dance, song and even love—pleasures sweeter than the gift of words—but of words themselves the heart is never tired"—*ma sazietà di lingua il cor non sente.* Leopardi was an unfulfilled, unhappy man and he exaggerates. But there is something in what he says.

GILLIAN EDWARDS

ACKNOWLEDGEMENTS

I acknowledge my gratitude to the following for permission to quote from copyright material:

P. J. Kenedy & Sons for *Butler's Lives of the Saints* (revised by H. Thurston, S.J., and Donald Attwater).

Harper & Row for Brewer's *Dictionary of Phrase and Fable*, by E. Cobham Brewer.

Mr George Scott Moncrieff and Random House, Inc. for *Remembrance of Things Past*, Vol. 1, by Marcel Proust, translated by C. K. Scott Moncrieff.

St Martin's Press for Grove's *Dictionary of Music and Musicians* (ed. E. Blom).

Oxford University Press for *The Oxford English Dictionary*, *The Oxford Dictionary of English Etymology* (ed. Onions), *An Etymological Dictionary of the English Language*, by W. W. Skeat, *The Oxford Dictionary of English Christian Names* (compiled by Withycombe), and *Italian Popular Comedy*, by K. M. Lea.

The Macmillan Company for *A Dictionary of the Underworld*, *Origins* and *A Dictionary of Slang*, all by Eric Partridge; Barnes & Noble, Inc. for Grose's *A Classical Dictionary of the Vulgar Tongue* (ed. Partridge); Hillary House Publishers, Ltd for *A Dictionary of British Surnames*, by P. H. Reaney.

The extracts from *Men at Arms* and *Love Among the Ruins*, by Evelyn Waugh, are reprinted by permission of Little, Brown & Co., and those from *Webster's Third New International Dictionary* 1961 by permission of G. & C. Merriam Co., publishers of the Merriam–Webster Dictionaries.

CONTENTS

I

BONJOUR, MONSIEUR PANTALON

Dictionaries, of course, can never be really up to date, since they deal with the written rather than the spoken language. Out of curiosity I consulted English and American standard works on the subject of *pants*; in 1959 the *OED*[1] said they were "men's drawers", in 1961 Webster[2] said they were "women's drawers". The *Concise Oxford*, also in 1959, decided to call them "long tight drawers", but also includes *panties*, "close fitting knickers worn by women". *Drawers* it defines as "a two-legged undergarment suspended from the waist".

Two interesting points arise. First, there seems to be no word to describe these garments that is not slang. Even drawers, respectable as it sounds, was originally "a term of low origin", given by Harman in the sixteenth century as "Peddelars Frenche" for "hosen", in the sense of something one draws on, and defined by Grose as "stockings". Second, the remarkably late appearance of this or any other word implying the existence of such an undergarment. Not till 1611 do we hear of "Draws or underhose of linnen", and in 1711 of the "Holland Drawers" of "country squires". Hose, with its old plural *hosen* (hoses are things with which to water the garden) is infinitely older, going back to pre-Conquest times. And it was with hose, "an article of clothing for the leg", that pants or pantaloons properly corresponded.

About 1730 *Chambers's Cyclopaedia* gave "Pantaloon or Pantalon" as "the name of an ancient garment frequent among our forefathers, consisting of breeches and stockings all of a piece. The de-

[1] *A New English Dictionary on Historical Principles*, Oxford University Press.
[2] *Webster's Third New International Dictionary*, G. and C. Merriam & Co.

nomination comes from the Venetians, who first introduced this
habit, and who are called Pantaloni." The author is on the right
track, but most of his statements are only doubtfully true. "An
ancient garment . . . made precisely to the form of (the) body,
and all of a piece from head to foot," as he goes on to say, was
certainly "frequent among our forefathers", and it may well have
come from Italy, since picture after picture by Renaissance
painters shows slim and brilliant young men encased from the
waist to the feet in what look like ballet tights. But while these
were fashionable they were never known as pantaloons; in Italy
they were *calze*, in England hose or hosen.

Doublet and hose was the usual wear for a man with any
pretence to fashion for at least two centuries, and as doublets got
shorter and shorter more of the hose was revealed. Chaucer's
Poor Parson, shocked by the indecency of this "horrible dis-
ordinat scantnesse of clothing", which he attributes to the sin of
pride, roundly denounces "thise cutted sloppes[1] or hainselins,[2]
that thrugh hir shortnesse ne covere nat the shameful membres of
man, to wikked entente. Allas! somme of hem shewen the boce[3]
of hir shap, and the horrible swollen membres, that semeth lyk
the maladie of hirnia, in the wrappinge of hir hoses; and eek the
buttokes of hem faren[4] as it were the hindre part of a she-ape in
the full of the mone."

As with most other criticisms of the fashions of the young and
the rich, however, disapproval proved no discouragement. This
kind of dress was certainly common at least until Shakespeare's
time, for Rosalind, disguised as a man, when she hears that her
lover Orlando has been seen in the forest of Arden, cries, "Alas
the day! What shall I do with my doublet and hose?" Nowadays,
of course, she needn't have worried, for according to James Laver
"the silhouette of a modern young woman" of 1967 in mini-

---

[1] loose over garments.   [2] short jackets.   [3] protuberance (boss).
                        [4] seem.

skirt and tights "is almost exactly that of a young man in (say) 1490".

In the same play Shakespeare speaks of:

> The lean and slipper'd Pantaloon,
> With spectacles on nose and pouch on side,
> His youthful hose well sav'd, a world too wide
> For his shrunk shank.

Pantaloon, the glossaries will tell you, represents a "foolish old man", "the lean, bespectacled, slippered dotard of Italian comedy." The hose have no connexion with the name, except that this type of costume denoted the character, just as a clown even now may have ruffles and a pointed hat. They are, as *Chambers's Cyclopaedia* goes on to say, "the habit or dress these buffoons usually wear."

As with so much else in the fifteenth and sixteenth centuries, Pantaloon, then, came out of Italy. He was one of the stock figures in that extraordinarily popular and long-lived dramatic form the *Commedia dell'Arte*. This type of performance seems to have risen to favour under the patronage of Pope Leo X Medici, particularly in Venice and Rome. There were no plays as we know them, only a series of plots or dramatic situations; a kind of film scenario without the dialogue. All the speech and much of the 'business' the actors improvised as they went along, and at this, from much practice, they were very skilled. Though the stories might differ, the characters were always the same: a pair or two pairs of lovers, scheming servants who engage in deceptions of incredible intricacy and provide most of the comic turns, scolding old women, tricksters of all kinds, and the heavy father types, the Doctor, the Captain (often Spanish), and the needy and seedy Pantaloon. To emphasise still more the artificial and impersonal quality of their parts the actors often wore masks, as was the custom in Greek and Roman times.

There had long been a vogue for amateur theatricals performed by aristocratic young courtiers in princely palaces. But these companies were strictly professional; their name shows that. *Arte* is the Italian word for a trade or craft, and the *Arti* were the great professional guilds that ruled Florence for so long. The actors were full-time, paid, and travelled about from place to place, even so far as France or England, much like the old stock companies or the modern ballet or opera. Nor was there any interchange of parts; a man was engaged for a particular character and stuck to it. Casanova, who should have known, since his mother certainly and his putative father were theatre people, remarked when he was in Paris in 1750 that no one seemed to know the actors' names: "At that time it was the custom in France to call the Italian actors by the name they had on the stage. *Bon jour, Monsieur Arlequin; bon jour, Monsieur Pantalon*: such was the manner in which the French used to address the actors who personified those characters." So the habit of identifying, say, Sean Connery with James Bond, is not entirely modern.

A contemporary account dated 1568 describes the actor playing Pantaloon: "From the other side of the stage appeared Messer Orlando dressed as a Magnifico in a crimson satin tunic, Venetian hose of scarlet, a long black mantle reaching to the ground and a mask that drew roars of laughter at first sight." *Magnifico* in Venice was the title of honour of a noble or a man of wealth or eminence; here it is mocking and ironic. Il Magnifico Messer Pantalone de' Bisognosi is the full style of the gentleman—The Magnificent Master Pantaloon the Needy. "His 'neediness'," says Lea in his study of *Italian Popular Comedy*, "may refer to his want of physique, of credit, of domestic consolation, or of authority." Certainly he was always losing something; his dignity, his children (who disappear in early youth, only to be rediscovered by fantastic coincidences), his daughter (who elopes, or marries the wrong man), his money, his jewels or anything

else he can be cheated out of. Shylock, finding Jessica has robbed
him and run off with Lorenzo, crying:

> My daughter! O my ducats! O my daughter!
> Fled with a Christian! O my Christian ducats!
> Justice! the law! my ducats and my daughter!

is a typical Pantaloon figure, except that Shakespeare's skill makes
him not a type but a person, and we share his grief.

But why Pantaloon, or in the Italian more usually Pantaleone?
Messer Orlando, we notice, wore Venetian hose; the character
was almost always played as a Venetian complete with dialect.
And he seems to have got that name as a Welshman might be
called David or an Irishman Patrick, because, according to Mahn,
"Saint Pantaleone was the patron saint of Venice (or rather a very
popular saint), and hence a baptismal name very frequent among
the Venetians, and applied to them by other Italians as a nickname." Byron knew it, for he speaks in *Childe Harold* of

> Her very by-word sprung from victory,
> The "Planter of the Lion", which through fire
> And blood she bore o'er subject earth and sea.

And he gives his own derivation of the word as Piantaleone,
"The Planter of the Lion . . . that is, the Lion of Saint Mark, the
standard of the Republic, which is the origin of the word
Pantaloon." But, says Skeat, "the etymology advocated by Lord
Byron is extraordinary and indeed ridiculous."

Venice had many contacts with the east, and Pantaleone was an
eastern saint. It is generally accepted that such a martyr did
actually exist, though nothing is known of him beyond legends
which are "valueless". Tradition says he came from Nicomedia
in Asia Minor, and though most authorities translate his name
as meaning 'all lion', Butler chooses an alternative spelling,
Pantaleimon or 'all compassionate'. This seems more appropriate

B

to the profession he followed, that of medicine, rising to become physican to the emperor Galerius Maximianus himself, who at that time divided the rule of the Empire with Diocletian.

As a Christian he was endangered when Diocletian's persecution broke out in Nicomedia in 303. Immediately he distributed all his possessions among his poor fellow Christians, and continued as he had always done to treat the sick without sending in any bills, which earned him the title of Holy Moneyless One. It also seems to have provoked the jealousy of other physicians in the town, who denounced him and he was arrested. In spite of the Emperor's interest on his behalf he refused to be saved, and was condemned to death. "He was subject to six different attempts to kill him, by burning, liquid lead, drowning, wild beasts, the wheel and the sword; all these, with the help of the Lord . . . he frustrated, till at length he permitted himself to be beheaded." One can't help feeling it was very magnanimous of him. 'All lion' he must have been—"What wouldst thou have of me? Good king of cats, nothing but one of your nine lives." Pantaloon doesn't much resemble his namesake: he is a comic, not a tragic figure, to be laughed at rather than with, but in spite of all his humiliations and misfortunes he usually wins out in the end.

Here then is Lea's description of the saint's successor: "Pantaleone comes on to the stage masked as a lean inquisitive old man; in his loose slippers he walks like a hen, one hand is thrust behind to hold back his *zimarra*, and except for this long black gown and for the little cap 'cowched fast to the pate like an oyster', as Gabriel Harvey has it, he is all in red; at his belt there is a knife for vengeance, a handkerchief for affecting recognition scenes, and often a pouch. Sometimes he peers through spectacles, and by the wag of his finger before his dialect is heard he has established himself as the Venetian."

For centuries it seemed that this character was all but immortal.

The *Commedia dell' Arte* or a travesty of it invaded many countries, especially France and England, where it was in constant demand in the form of the Harlequinade or pantomime. Harlequinades were performed right up till Victorian times, either as curtain raisers or as farces to follow a more serious play and send the audience home in a happy mood. In pantomime we have perhaps the last vestiges of it, though the principal boy wears the tights and Pantaloon might seem to have been transformed into the Dame as "the butt of the clown's jokes and his abettor in his pranks and tricks." Harlequin, apparently, may descend from the legendary French *Herlichini* or *maisniée Hellequin*, those devilish hunters and their hounds who sweep through Europe on the storm-winds and carry off the damned to hell. And pantomime has no connexion with Pantaloon. The Greek *panto-mimos* or imitator of all, was a kind of mime or ballet dancer, interpreting in dumb show the whole development of a story or plot, first to the accompaniment of a flute-player and a singer, later of a chorus and orchestra.

Strangely enough it is not until the fashion for tight hose had long been dead that men's nether garments were referred to as pantaloons. These were an extravagant style of rather full breeches, something like voluminous plus-fours, which came into vogue with Charles II. Bell, in a note to *Hudibras*, says, "The pantaloon belongs to the Restoration. It was loose in the upper part and puffed, and covered the legs, the lower part terminating in stockings ('breeches and stockings,' in fact, 'all of a piece'). In an inventory of the time . . . pantaloons are mentioned, and a yard and a half of lute-string allowed for them."

As with most other novelties, they were imported from the Continent; not Italy but France. According to the diarist Evelyn the French *haut ton* had copied the idea from the exaggerated costume of the stage comedians of the period, hence the name: "When the freak takes our Monsieurs to appear like so many

Farces or Jack-puddings on the stage." They were also called petticoat breeches because their fullness and the frills with which they were often adorned gave them the appearance of women's skirts and led to ambiguous jokes about the sex of the wearer. "I would choose," Evelyn adds, "some fashion not so pinching as to need a shooing horn with the Dons" (that is the Spaniards, who still wore their small-clothes so tight they looked, as we would say, as if they had been poured into them), "nor so exorbitant as the Pantaloons, which are a kind of Hermaphrodite and of neither sex." Always a little *outré*, the fashion for them soon passed, though Defoe remembers them in 1719. Anyone who has seen the traditional drawings of Robinson Crusoe in his home-made suit of goat's leather has a very good idea of the style of these garments: "The breeches were made of the skin of an old he-goat, whose hair hung down to such a length . . . that, like pantaloons, it reached to the middle of my legs."

Under the first three Georges sober breeches, comfortably fitting and fastened at the knee, were the common wear. In the late eighteenth and early nineteenth centuries, however, they began to creep down the leg until they reached mid-calf, fastened by ribbons or buttons. By 1812 they were down to the ankle, with straps under the instep to keep them in place and stop them from wrinkling, very much after the style of the 'stretch pants' women wear today. Again they were known as pantaloons or trousers, a word borrowed from the Gaelic *triubhas*, trews or 'trowzes'. This was the name given from the sixteenth century to "the nether garments of the Irish", who wore "little coats and strait breeches called trouses". A jest-book of 1630 says, "A jellous wife is like an Irish trouze, alwayes close to a man's tail." Our modern spelling *trousers* does not appear till the eighteenth century, probably on the pattern of drawers. These garments were loosely fitting and were worn first by sailors and then by soldiers, perhaps for ease of movement.

Like most other new styles, they were considered definitely not
'the thing', and condemned as improper and even indecent,
though it is difficult to see why. Cambridge University strongly
disapproved: "In October 1812 an order was made by Saint
John's and Trinity College that every young man who appeared in
Hall or Chapel in pantaloons or trousers should be considered
absent." And quoting the rhyme:

> Nothing so bewitches
> As boots and leather breeches,

a contributor to *Notes and Queries* reported, "My father went up
to Cambridge in 1794. In his undergraduate days a strong attempt
was made to put down 'pantaloons' by the Vice-Chancellor,
master of—as it was then called—Catharine Hall. When he
appeared in public he used to be saluted by the undergraduates—
from some safe place, we will suppose—with the following
couplet:

> Od zoons, odd zoons,
> Lowther Yates and Pantaloons."

By 1816, however, Captain Gronow found that in Paris
"knee-breeches were only worn by a few old fogies: trousers and
shoes being the usual costume of all the young men of the day."
So when he attended a party in London he went "dressed *à la
française* . . . with white neck-cloth and waistcoat, and black
trousers, shoes and silk stockings." But soon he was tapped on the
shoulder and told that the Prince Regent considered his appearing
"without kneebreeches" showed "a want of proper respect" and
he was forced to leave. Lord Frederick Bentinck consoled him by
saying, "Depend on it, Gronow, the Prince, who is a lover of
novelty, will wear trousers himself before the year is out, and then
you may laugh at him." This prediction was proved true in less
than a month, when Gronow met the Regent at a ball "dressed

exactly as I had been"—and from then on trousers were respectable even at Court.

In England *trousers* superseded the earlier *pantaloons*. In America the older word was commonly retained, but since it took too long to say it was soon shortened to *pants*. Though recognised as being a vulgar abbreviation—Oliver Wendell Holmes called it "a word not made for gentlemen but 'gents'"—like many other vulgarisms it became so embedded in the language that its origin was almost forgotten. Pants, people nowadays would tell you on both sides of the Atlantic, are trousers, not pantaloons. Except, of course, when they are drawers.

Meanwhile, even more daringly, the women were wearing them. Skirts by about 1825 had lifted a little off the ground, and smart young girls showed peeping underneath "loose drawers or trousers with a frill at the bottom of each leg," known by the linguistically horrible but determinedly feminine name of *pantalettes*. These led on to what was described in America as the "graceful and becoming" Bloomer costume of "frock and pants", "a female costume consisting of a short skirt and loose trousers gathered closely round the ankle, so called from Mrs Amelia Bloomer of New York, who tried in 1849 to introduce the fashion."

Contrary to general belief, Mrs Bloomer "did not invent it, was not the first to wear it, and protested against its being called by her name." According to Blackwell, that honour should go to "Mrs Elizabeth Smith Miller, the daughter of Gerrit Smith . . . a great landowner in western New York. Mrs Miller wanted a dress in which she could easily take long walks about her country home," unhampered by voluminous skirts that trailed in the mud. She designed for herself "a small jacket, a full skirt descending a little below the knee, and trousers down to the ankle. It was not beautiful, but was very comfortable and convenient and entirely modest."

Amelia Bloomer's name became associated with this costume because, as editor of what is described as "the first woman's paper", called *The Lily: a Ladies' Journal, devoted to Temperance and Literature*, she publicised it and praised it highly. As *The Illustrated London News* remarked in 1851, "*The Lily* appears to be ostensibly devoted to the advocacy of the new fashion, conducive to health by avoidance of damp skirts hanging about the feet and ankles, since they would be clad in a boot . . . the very things for American sloughs and slosh."

These comments were occasioned by "a lecture upon Bloomers" delivered at the Literary Institution, Fitzroy-square, on 15 and 22 September, "the lecturer, of course, wearing the new attire, of black satin, consisting of a jacket, a skirt scarcely reaching to the knee, and a pair of very wide trousers, tied at the ankle." That Mrs Bloomer's advocacy was warm can be seen from her reply to ladies of sixty inquiring if they could wear such a costume with decorum. "Do just as your impulses move you to do," she wrote. "What you find a burden in belief or apparel, cast off. Fit yourselves for a higher sphere, and cease grovelling in this dirt. Let there be no stain of earth upon your soul or your apparel." Girls nowadays have taken almost too literally this advice; it would be interesting to know her opinion of bikinis.

As for the bloomers that one inadvertently makes, these have nothing to do with the lady. This bloomer is most probably a shortening of "blooming error", where blooming "is used as one of the many slang euphemistic substitutes for bloody." The long rounded bread loaf of the same name, however, I would venture to suggest was so called because of its shape; it much resembles one leg of "a pair of very wide trousers" gathered at the bottom to fit.

London, while cautiously adopting the Bloomer costume, seems not entirely to have approved of the name. The *Daily News* in 1897 suggested that for bicycle riding "there are very pretty possibilities with a short skirt and pantalettes," while the horsewoman might canter out in "pantaloons of chamois leather, buttoning close at the ankles." But soon these outer garments became trousers even for women, pantalettes shrank and shrank into pants, often known as briefs, and the roomy bloomers, now with elastic round the knees, almost disappeared. So Amelia Bloomer and poor Saint Pantaleone share the same cruel fate, to be remembered only by ladies' and gents' unmentionables!

2

A TALENT FOR FARCE

What is a French farce? The answer is not so simple as it sounds. It may depend on whether you are an inveterate theatre-goer, a culinary expert or a student of mediaeval liturgical music.

Perhaps we should start with cookery. "Forcemeat, or farcemeat as it was originally called," says the 1961 version of Mrs Beeton, "derives its name from the French verb *farcir*, to stuff." Constance Spry is more explicit: "Roughly one might say that forcemeats and stuffings in English are mixtures used as accompaniments to and fillings for certain main foods, such as poultry, game, fish, meat and vegetables, while the French farces are extended to cover, for instance, quenelles, mousselines and creams accompanying an elaborate dish or served as a course apart." But most of us don't bother. We only remember about the older name when, licking through the index of the cookery book with a hasty finger, we try *Stuffing* and curse because it merely says *See Forcemeat*.

The original word, then, is *farce*, from Old French *farsir*, French *farcir* (hence considerable confusion about whether it should be spelt with *s* or *c*), Latin *farcire*, meaning to stuff, to fill full of something. Also to cram the stomach, so a glutton might farce himself with food, or to fill out what is lean or shrunken, so Pantaloon needed a little more flesh to farce his "youthful hose" that were "a world too wide For his shrunk shank." It can even be used to describe the custom of embalming, as in 1563, "They bury dead bodies farced with spices."

But the spices with which it is usually associated are kitchen ones. Chickens and meat are farced when they are stuffed with force-meat, herbs, etc. "Broche thin pygge: then farce him," was

13

perhaps the fifteenth-century equivalent of "First catch your hare . . . " Such spices and seasonings were very necessary, not so much to bring out the flavour of the meat as to disguise it. Most of the animals were killed in the autumn and the joints salted down; by the end of winter they were rather tough and rather high. Even when meat could be got fresh the taste for such garnishings remained. "Make a farce with the livers minced small," says Mrs Hannah Glasse, among other elaborate recipes, in 1796. And our Christmas bird still has to have its stuffing.

About the noun *farcemeat* or *forcemeat*, as it came to be known by the confusion of *farce* with *force*, there seems a certain lack of clarity. The *OED* defines it as "meat chopped fine, spiced and highly seasoned, chiefly used for stuffing or as a garnish." This would seem to apply to a ham or giblet stuffing, but not to one made with herbs. Holmes in 1688 maintained that "forcemeat is a Meat with a stuffing of Herbs or other things made to that purpose," thus apparently including the whole dish, stuffing and all. Usually, however, we think of it not as a dish of meat that has been farced, nor as meat for forcing into, say, a chicken, but rather as the stuffing or farce itself. Nor need it be made with meat, for *meat* meant merely some kind of food.

As for the alteration of *farce* to *force*, the *OED* accounts for this with the suggestion that "in the fifteenth century cookery books *aforce* is often used in the same context as *farce*; in some passages the sense may be 'to strengthen' (as by adding gravy), 'to season, or to spice'." Because of the similarity in spelling and meaning the two could be easily interchanged.

The general sense of farce, then, is to put something in that was not there before, to pad out, to interpolate, to interlard—another kitchen metaphor. "Other prodigious miracles he farseth into his storie," says Purchas in 1613; that is, he drags them in where they have no right to be, to colour or 'spice' his tale. The mediaeval mind had a passion for elaboration and ornament; you

need only look at the great Gothic cathedrals to see that. And
this betrayed them into the liturgical farce, remote ancestor of
all those odd goings-on we sometimes watch on the stage.

As early as the eighth and ninth centuries musical settings of
the Mass had become involved and intricate. Words and phrases
in the Kyrie, the Gloria and so on were drawn out and lengthened,
soon there grew up, says Grove,[1] "a custom of making inter-
polations into the church chant, which in course of time spread
through almost the whole range of liturgical song. Such inter-
polations had the generic name of *trope*," from Latin *tropus*, a
figure of speech, Greek *tropos*, turn.

The longer and more elaborate these tropes grew, the more
difficult it was for the singers to remember them, especially as
there was no clear system of musical notation for writing them
down. "Soon a need arose for words to be found to these . . .
intercalated *vocalizzi*, and then the habit came in of intercalating
words as well as music. The words were often either added to the
already existing music, or both words and music arose together
. . . As the development went on there was little left that had
not suffered from these parasites," the two exceptions being the
Credo and the Gospel, because of their particularly sacred nature.

In the Kyrie for instance, various phrases were interpolated
between *kyrie* and *eleison*, as *Kyrie, genitor ingenite, vera essentia,
eleison*, somewhat in the form of a litany. It was also common to
repeat a scriptural text or other words between the verses or after
every two verses of a psalm or canticle. This practice of inter-
larding or 'stuffing' was known as *farsing*, and the extraneous
material inserted into the liturgical chants as a *farse* (Latin *farsa*,
farsia) or *farce*.

Even the Epistle was farced; an *Epistola farcita* sounds quite
an elaborate affair. "Expository and hortatory passages" in the
vernacular, and sometimes it seems in rhyme, "were inserted

[1] Grove's *Dictionary of Music and Musicians*.

between the Latin sentences in chanting the epistle," thus "forming an explication or paraphrase of the Latin text, verse by verse, for the benefit of the people. A sub-deacon first repeated each verse of the epistle or *Lectio* in Latin, and two choristers sang a farse or explanation." The Council of Trent, however, disapproved of this practice as of many others. "True farcing," says the *Catholic Dictionary*, "was entirely mediaeval, and has now been abolished in the Roman rite."

Rather unexpectedly it left its name behind. Drama in England, as most people know, began with simple representations of the Gospel stories, acted in church. There is extant an account of one of the earliest of these, drawn up by Aethelwold, Bishop of Winchester, in the tenth century, showing how the monks of the cathedral acted out the lesson of Easter, telling that "the Lord is risen", taking the parts of "the angel sitting in the monument and the women with spices coming to anoint the body of Jesus," and making the appropriate responses.

This is not much more than a particularly elaborate 'farce' in the liturgical sense. By the thirteenth century true if elementary plays were performed, centred especially round the Christmas story. Such is the *Interfectio Puerorum* or Slaughter of the Innocents, as described by Pollard: "The part of the Holy Innocents was taken by the choirboys, the other characters, including the women, would be played by the clergy. In one part of the church . . . is erected a manger; in another a throne for Herod; a distant corner is supposed to represent Egypt . . . The story is set forth in the fewest possible words, interspersed with anthems for the choristers." So were born the Mysteries, which "deal with Gospel events only," and the Miracle Plays, which "are concerned with incidents derived from the legends of the saints of the Church."

Soon the plays moved out of the churches and on to the public greens or open streets. They were no longer acted solely by the clergy, but by ordinary people of the town, craftsmen and members of trade guilds, assisted perhaps by any wandering jugglers, minstrels and professional entertainers who happened to be in the district. The subjects were still religious, still portrayed with delight and simple reverence, yet a need was soon felt for some little light relief. Perhaps to hold the attention of the audience, perhaps to give scope to the tumblers and fools, it became customary for a certain amount of comic business, an "interlude of impromptu buffoonery", to be inserted into the more serious text. *Cy est interposé une farsse*, says a fourteenth century French account of such a play; here, in other words, they put in something, pad it out. That these extempore 'farces' continued to be popular over a considerable period, sharpened and refined no doubt by the advent of the *Commedia dell'Arte*, we know from Shakespeare. "Let those that play your clowns speak no more than is set down for them", urges Hamlet. Putting in one's own gags is "villainous, and shows most pitiful ambition in the fool that uses it."

One of the first of these interludes to be written down comes in the Townley Play of the Shepherds; here it is not extraneous but part of a dramatic whole. Primus, Secundus and Tertius Pastor are watching their sheep in the fields; to them enters Mak, whom they suspect of being a sheep-stealer. Quite rightly too, for when they fall asleep he makes off with "a fatt shepe . . . a good flese . . . this wille I borrow." His goodwife Gylle, however, is afraid he will be followed, found out and hanged. Hide it in the cradle, she says, "to thay be gone . . . And I shalle lyg besyde in chylbed and grone." When the shepherds eventually come to search for their sheep Mak greets them with, "Syrs, drynkys," explaining that his wife "was lyght of a knave[1] childe this nyght" and should not be disturbed. They search and find nothing; somewhat ashamed they turn to go, then remember

[1] boy.

they have not complied with the custom of giving presents to a new-born child. Whereupon they crowd round the cradle and discover "a hornyd lad . . . What the dewille is this? he has a long snowte . . . He is lyke to oure shepe." So the theft is revealed and Mak tossed in a blanket. Satisfied, they return to the fields, only to be led by an angel to another new-born child lying "in a cryb fulle poorely Betwyx two bestys." This time they bring out their gifts, the best they can offer: "a bob of cherys," a bird and "a balle: Have and play the with alle And go to the tenys."

Once the drama was secularised comic pieces or farces were performed as separate plays and the origin of the name forgotten. Among the earliest remaining are those of John Heywood, dating from the beginning of the sixteenth century; these include such titles as *The Four PP: a very mery enterlude of a Palmer, a Pardoner, a Potecary and a Pedlar,* and *A mery Play between the Pardoner and the Frere, the Curate and neybour Pratte,* where everyone ends up fighting everyone else. Heywood was a Catholic and narrowly escaped being hanged for his faith; nevertheless his criticism of the Church and the clergy is scathing. This is characteristic of mediaeval farce which, says Chambers, was remarkable for "its free handling of contemporary life, the outspokenness, which often becomes indecency, of its language (and) its note of satire, especially towards the priest and other institutions deserving of reverence"—in fact much more like a late night show on the BBC than the fun and games at one time to be seen at the Aldwych or Whitehall theatres.

By the time Pepys in 1668 went "to the King's House, to see the first day of Lacy's 'Monsieur Ragou,' a farce," the satire had lost its sting and amusement predominated. "By Farce I understand that species of the drama whose sole aim and tendency is to excite laughter," asserted Hurd in 1756, and from that day to this no one has quarrelled with his definition. Farce, says *The*

Oxford Companion to the Theatre, is "an extreme form of comedy in which laughter is raised at the expense of probability, particularly by horse-play and bodily assault." People knocking other people about and losing their trousers are always funny; in this respect at least we have never grown up and probably never shall.

As for the horse-play, that seems once to have been quite literal. "We have a play wherein we use a horse," says one of Middleton's characters in 1627. Dryden is more explicit: "They get upon their jennets and prance before their ladies' windows . . . This horse-play they call making love." So it started as theatrical horsemanship, designed to impress, and gradually descended to our sense of rough or boisterous play; "awkward overturns of glasses, plates and salt-cellars," as Lord Chesterfield remarked with repugnance of behaviour at his dinner-table in 1749.

In ancient Rome such comic plays, called *Atellane*, were extremely popular; "the favourite theme, which is common indeed to farce of all ages, was that of conjugal infidelity," and some of them were exceedingly indecent. Here again we haven't changed very much. "In modern use the word *farce* is applied to a full-length play dealing with some absurd situation, hanging generally upon extramarital relations, hence the term 'bedroom farce'." Or, if you prefer it, French farce, which is where we came in.

Farce also has a metaphorical sense, describing something ridiculous, "a proceeding that is ludicrously futile or insincere, a hollow pretence, a mockery." "'Tis all with him a Farce and all a Ladle,' as a very facetious poet says," remarks Wotton in 1705. The "facetious poet" was Matthew Prior, who had just published *The Ladle* among other pleasing verses. It tells how Jove and Mercury descend to earth and visit a farmer and his wife:

You have tonight beneath your roof
A pair of gods (nay, never wonder),
This youth can fly and I can thunder.
I'm Jupiter and he Mercurius,
My page, my son indeed, but spurious.

Out of their benevolence they grant the pair three wishes.
The woman, Corisca, cries:

A ladle for our silver dish
Is what I want, is what I wish.

The husband, disgusted, shouts at her:

What should be great you turn to farce;
I wish the ladle in your arse!

Whereupon:

The ladle fell into the room
And stuck in old Corisca's bum.

They have had two wishes and are forced to use the last

To ease the woman's awkward pain
And get the ladle out again.

Prior had quite a talent for this gay, irreverent kind of satire. As for *talent*, that too is a metaphor, so old we have most of us forgotten it ever had any other meaning.

We borrowed the word from Latin *talenta*, plural of *talentum*, which comes from Greek *talenton*. This was originally a measure of weight used throughout most of the ancient world, and particularly among the Babylonians, Assyrians, Greeks and Romans. It has been estimated at values ranging from fifty-six to eighty-eight English pounds; certainly it was of quite considerable size. Just as we have pounds avoirdupois and pounds

sterling, the talent soon came to stand for a sum of money, the approximate worth of a talent weight of gold or silver. Evidence that it was known very early in England comes from the Anglo-Saxon King Alfred, speaking in 893 of "twa hund talentana."

During the Middle Ages it acquired throughout the Romance languages a somewhat unexpected secondary meaning of "inclination of mind, will, wish, desire, appetite," even lust. So Caxton writes, "Great talent and desyre she had to know him." And as a piece of jargon it seems to have been very popular with falconers, rules being laid down for giving hawks a 'talent' for their food, or for flying, and so on. Sometimes it is qualified as an ill talent or maltalent—"To his ost sone he went Ful of ire and maltalent"—but on the principle that bad meanings drive out the good, even its simple use in this sense is most often opprobrious.

It was, of course, the translation of the Bible that set the word off on its modern career. Here is Wyclif in 1382: "As a man goyinge fer in pilgrimage, clepide[1] his servauntis and bitoke[2] to hem his goodis; and to oon he gave five talents, forsothe to an other two." And so the familiar tale unfolds. He who had received five talents "went and traded with the same, and made them other five talents. And likewise he that had received two, he also gained other two. But he that had received one went and digged in the earth, and hid his lord's money." At last the lord comes home and calls his servants to him. To the first two he is gracious, praising them: "Well done, thou good and faithful servant; thou hast been faithful over a few things, I will make thee ruler over many things: enter into the joy of thy lord." But for him who brings back only what he was given, "Thou wicked and slothful servant . . . thou oughtest . . . to have put my money to the exchangers, and then . . . I should have received mine own with usury." So his one talent is taken from him and

---

[1] called.　　　　　　　　　　　[2] entrusted.

c

given to the man with ten, according to that most unsocialistic of all texts, "For unto everyone that hath shall be given, and he shall have abundance; but from him that hath not shall be taken away even that which he hath." And the unprofitable servant is cast "into outer darkness" among the "weeping and gnashing of teeth."

This, like much else in the teaching of Jesus, is a hard saying, but its lesson is clear. It has, of course, always been interpreted allegorically, the talents implying the gifts of God "to every man according to his several ability." So writing in 374 Saint Jerome cries, *Vae illi, qui acceptum talentum in sudario ligans*—Woe to the man who receives a talent and ties it in a napkin! From his phraseology it is clear that he is thinking in terms of money, and consciously turning it to metaphorical use. The napkin comes from Saint Luke's version of the story, which though a little confused has a much more modern ring. Here ten servants are given a pound each (Greek *mna* or *mina*); one of them brings it back saying, "Lord, behold, here is thy pound, which I kept laid up in a napkin." Whereupon he is chidden for not having put it "into the bank", where he might at least have got "usury" or interest.

What did these servants actually receive? The answer of course can be only very approximate, and Bible renderings give us no help. With one exception, all the English translations I have consulted, even the *Bible in Basic English*, stick to Wyclif's original *talent*, though the *New English Bible* substitutes rather arbitrarily "a bag of gold". There seems no doubt that what is involved is not just a few coins, but a very large sum of money. When the talent is mentioned in the Old Testament it concerns usually the payment of tribute or taxes, or the price of particularly important goldsmith's work, as for instance when Solomon's Temple was "overlaid with fine gold . . . the beams, the posts, and the walls thereof, and the doors thereof . . .

amounting to six hundred talents." This would be a talent of gold, the value of which has been put as high as £5,000 or £6,000 in modern money. By New Testament times it had been superseded in general use by the talent of silver, containing 6,000 Greek drachmae; recent estimates place it at between £250–£350, or about 1,000 dollars. No wonder the poor man was afraid of losing it and buried it in the garden.

Shakespeare, rather surprisingly, uses all three meanings of the word. In *Timon of Athens*, which is of course set in Greece, the talent is a unit of currency. Timon, the rich and generous man, whose creditors have suddenly decided to foreclose and ruin him, sends a servant to remind Ventidius that

> When he was poor . . .
> Imprison'd and in scarcity of friends,
> I clear'd him with five talents.

He wants the money back, but of course it does not come. In *Cymbeline* Iachimo, who has taken a bet with Posthumus Leonatus that he will seduce his wife, tells her hypocritically that he accounts her his (her husband's) "beyond all talents," meaning evil inclinations, passions, lusts. Yet much earlier we have the pedantical Holofernes, praised for his alliterative verses—"a rare talent"—which he mock-modestly disclaims with, "This is a gift that I have, simple, simple . . . But the gift is good . . . and I am thankful for it."

Already by the sixteenth century, and even more so in the seventeenth, when the King James Bible was published, this sense of a gift from God, "mental endowment, natural ability, power or ability of mind or body viewed as something divinely entrusted to a person for use or improvement," had ousted all the others. "Talents" says Wynkyn de Worde in 1531, "that God hath lent to a man in this lyfe, of the whiche he will aske moost strayte accounte." And a century before Lydgate had

cried out, "Who shal me save Fro feendys daunger, t'accounte
for my talent?" The same fear, though expressed with more
sophistication, troubled Milton in his blindness:

> And that one Talent which is death to hide,
> Lodg'd with me useless, though my Soul more bent
> To serve therewith my Maker, and present
> My true account least he returning chide.

But he concludes with typical Miltonic loftiness that

> God doth not need
> Either man's work or his own gifts . . .
> They also serve who only stand and waite.

This idea that talent is something with which we are 'endowed'
and for which we shall one day be expected to 'account' is very
firmly entrenched in the language. "Remember," says Charles
Kingsley sternly, "that your talents are a loan from God." And
the need to improve or cultivate our talents remains like a
haunting guilt even with those of us who would deny that God
ever gave us anything. They are there and ought to be made use
of. "Talent," says a modern American writer, "is a wishy-
washy thing unless . . . solidly founded on honest hard work."
   Though the conception of talent is particularly associated
with creative or artistic skill, one can have a talent for anything
from playing the violin or conjuring or cookery to what T. S.
Eliot once called "ingratitude or unsociability." In modern use,
like so many other words, it has completely lost its edge. It
can mean no more than general intelligence or mental power;
Coleridge first put forward the idea of an "aristocracy of talent".
It can also mean "talent as embodied in the talented," either
the skill itself or the person who possesses it. So we have talent
scouts, whose job it is to "discover and recruit people of talent
for a specialised field or activity," whether it is football, ballet

or electioneering. And when a film actress is described as "one of Hollywood's most luscious talents" it is tempting to wonder what exactly is hidden or not hidden in that napkin.

In the late eighteenth century, particularly in Germany and France, talent acquired another association, almost entirely unrelated to its origin, the somewhat invidious contrast with genius. Genius is also inborn, but on a different plane from talent; it is "native intellectual power of an exalted type; an instinctive and extraordinary capacity for imaginative creation, original thought, invention or discovery." The word which is equated with the *genie* or *djinn* of Arabian mythology, once meant a tutelary deity or spirit, a demon or *daimon*, in the more expressive Greek, and a genius gives the impression of being a man possessed, having "that particular kind of intellectual power which has the appearance of proceeding from a supernatural inspiration . . . and which seems to arrive at its results in an inexplicable and miraculous manner."

Talent is a pleasant and enjoyable thing to have; it ought to be cultivated and can be improved by study and by practice. But no man buries genius in the earth or puts it out to usury; it is much more likely to rage through him like a fire and burn him up. "Carlyle's definition of genius," says Sir Ernest Gowers, "as meaning 'transcendent capacity of taking trouble, first of all,' provoked from Samuel Butler the comment that 'it might be more fitly described as a supreme capacity for getting its possessors into trouble of all kinds and keeping them therein so long as the genius remains'." Somehow we feel it would be unfair to bring genius to an accountant's reckoning or an auditor's scrutiny; if it brings its own rewards it also sends in its own bills, and often collapses into bankruptcy. "Well done, thou good and faithful servant," has a sense of irrelevance, inadequacy, even of anticlimax here.

Johnson does not recognise this meaning of the word in his

Dictionary; it had almost certainly not then developed what is now its most common interpretation. Even if he knew it he might not have entirely approved. He would never have thought of himself as possessing genius, except perhaps by Carlyle's definition. It was to help him accept his responsibilities that he wrote his Lexicographer's Prayer: "O God, who has hitherto supported me, enable me to proceed in this labour, and in the whole task of my present state; that when I shall render up, at the last day, an account of the talent committed to me, I may receive pardon, for the sake of Jesus Christ, Amen."

3

NECKLACES AND BEADS

"Come," says Mopsa to the shepherd's son at the sheep-shearing feast, "You promised me a tawdry lace and a pair of sweet gloves." And she had expensive tastes, she wasn't asking for anything cheap and gawdy. She might, if *The Winter's Tale* had been written earlier, have called it Saint Audrey's lace, Audrey being a shortened form of Etheldreda. These necklets, particularly fashionable in the sixteenth and seventeenth centuries, were sold in memory of the saint. As always happens, fashion trickled down from the rich to the poor; cheap imitations were made, tawdry laces became common, stylish women gave up wearing them, and finally *tawdry* acquired its modern meaning of "showy but worthless, having too much or ill-judged ornament."

What was Saint Audrey's lace and why was it so called? Ivor Brown says, "The usual explanation is that Saint Audrey believed herself to be punished for wearing rich jewellery round her neck: accordingly she took to wearing a collar of fine lace as a precautionary and ethical device." But this, if not downright misleading, is no more than half a tale. Etheldreda, though born a princess, is best remembered as a nun and nuns don't wear lace collars. Nor, as a rule, did Anglo-Saxon ladies. Saint Audrey's lace was surely something quite different from what we mean by the word. And so it proved to be.

Etheldreda, daughter of the king of East Anglia and therefore a political asset in a troubled country, was twice married, both times against her inclination, since she wanted only to take the veil, and both times the marriage remained unconsummated.

27

Her first husband, Tonbert, died, leaving her in possession of
the Isle of Ely, which he had presented to her as a wedding
gift. Her second husband, Ecgfrid, later king of Northumbria,
wishing to establish his dynasty, had understandably little
patience with a woman who was prepared to be a wife in name
only. But he got no support from his bishops and it was with the
help and encouragement of Wilfrid of York that Etheldreda
eventually left him. Though he pursued her, a river in sudden
spate cut him off and he had to let her go. Almost alone, she
travelled the length of England to her land at Ely, where she
founded a religious house. It was a double monastery, providing
for both monks and nuns, and she ruled it until her death in 679.

It is true she did have some strange ideas about dress. "After
the time that she went to the monastery," says Bede, "she
would never wear any linen but only woollen clothes, and seldom
wash herself in warm baths save against solemn high feasts, as
Easter, Whitsun or Twelfthtide, and then she would be the
last of all." That is, she bathed in the water after everyone else
had used it. But a hot bath has always been a luxury; our
ancestors never equated being clean with being godly.

Not till she lay dying do we hear about the necklaces. Bede,
who did his best to authenticate his history, talked to Cynifrid,
her physician. From him he learned that she had "a very great
swelling under her armpit, and they bade me, quoth he, to lance
the swelling, that the ill humour that was within might issue
out." In spite of his efforts, however, she died three days later.
And during this time, "when she was grieved with the foresaid
swelling and pain of her cheekbone and neck, she took great joy
in this kind of disease and was wont to say: I know most
certainly that I worthily do bear this burden of pain in my neck,
in which I remember that when I was a girl I did bear the superfluous and vain burden of tablets and ouches, and I believe that
the sovereign pity of God doth therefore send me this grief and

pain in my neck, that he may so absolve and acquit me from that guilt of vanity and lightness, whereas now instead of gold and precious stones the red fire heat and burning swelling breaketh out of my neck." But nothing is said about her wearing lace instead.

Tablets and ouches—Thomas Stapleton is translating with typical Elizabethan exuberance, which never used one word where it could get in two, the Latin *monile*, a necklace or collar. *Tablets* were tablet or more properly table diamonds, stones cut with a large flat upper surface surrounded by small facets, and often worn as rings or pendants. *Ouches*, on the other hand, were brooches, ornamental buckles or the sort of jewelled clasps that might be used to fasten a cloak. Because of their swelling shape the word could also mean a tumour or a sore on the skin, just as a carbuncle can be a ruby or a fiery pimple. So it is possible Stapleton, again in the true Elizabethan style, is punning here.

It is about the time this translation was being made that we first hear of tawdry lace. The Archdeacon of Canterbury in the reign of Mary Tudor quotes Bede's story and adds, "Our women of England are wont to wear about the neck a certain necklace formed of thin and fine silk, perchance in memory of what we have been told." He too writes in Latin, and his word for necklace is *torques*, properly a twisted collar. Certainly these "ties, fringes or bands", as they were later described, bore no resemblance to what we think of as a necklace or as lace.

Indeed they take us back to the time when a 'neck lace' was apt to be fatal to the body rather than to the soul. A lace is a loop, so a snare or a trap, the very *laqueum* or noose with which the Vulgate says Judas hanged himself. Later it came to mean a cord or a string, especially when used as a fastening—boot-laces, in fact, or those long strings with which ladies once laced themselves into their stays. So tawdry laces were some kind of silk ties, soft and fine and knotted round the neck. No identifiable picture of them seems to exist, so we can only imagine what the effect must have been.

They could, however, like men's neckties and some versatile modern jewellery, also be used as belts. Spenser, urging "shepheards daughters" to make themselves fit to appear before the Queen, tells them:

> See, that your rudenesse doe not you disgrace;
>> Binde your fillets faste,
>> And gird in your waste,
> For more finesse, with a tawdrie lace.

It sounds like a sixteenth-century recipe for slimming. Clearly the laces were still considered very smart, but as high fashion they had had their day. In 1616 Rich is bemoaning the "happy age when a man might have wooed his wench with a pair of kid-leather gloves, a silver thimble, or with a tawdry lace; but now a velvet gown, a chain of pearl, or a coach with four horses, will scarcely serve the turn."

On or about 17 October every year a fair was held at Ely "in the fane of Saint Etheldreda". Quite naturally tawdry laces were sold there, and equally naturally the quality and the price began to go down, so that everyone could afford these souvenirs. By 1706 the word *tawdry* was being defined as "tricked up with such tinsel stuff or lace as is usually sold at Audery-Fair in Cambridgeshire." From this it sounds as if the 'lace' may have become the kind of braid made of loops of gold and silver wire by then much used for trimming clothes, especially men's. Nothing tarnishes or grows shabby more quickly than imitation glitter, cheap and nasty.

Tinsel, in fact, has had a similar history. It comes from the French *étincelle*, a spark or a flash of fire, and was used to describe fabrics made to sparkle and shine by interweaving them with gold or silver thread. Once again cheap imitation killed their value and the word came to mean something showy or attractive with little intrinsic worth. Though perhaps from its association with Christmas and the stage it retains an endearing quality which tawdry decidedly lacks.

For the origin of this word Francis Grose at the end of the eighteenth century proposed an explanation all his own. He defines it as "garish, gawdy with lace or staring and discordant colours" and says it is to be derived "from the shrine and altar of Saint Audrey (an Isle of Ely saintess), which for finery exceeded all others thereabouts, so as to become proverbial; whence any fine dressed man or woman was said to be all Saint Audrey, and by contraction all tawdry." He has the right idea but seems never to have heard of the famous lace.

About a hundred years later a Canon of Ely, Charles Stubbs, in his *Historical Memorials* came forward with still another story. He quotes from the *Liber Eliensis* the legend of a certain Brytstan of Caterict (or Chatteris) who, being wrongfully imprisoned in the reign of Henry I, prayed to the saint to help him. By her intervention his chains were snapped in two, and having told his tale to the Queen he was allowed to go free. He became a monk at Ely and hung up his chains as a kind of *ex voto* offering, before the altar of the church, where they remained for many centuries.

Consequently it became, says Stubbs, a custom of the convent to give "to the pilgrims who flocked to Saint Awdrey's Shrine . . . in memory of this miracle and of the virtues of Saint Awdrey, and as a memento of their visit to Ely, miniature shackles like those of Brytstan. These are 'the Saint Awdry's chains' which at a later time had degenerated into plaited ribands, and are still (i.e., in 1897) to be bought among the *t'awdry* finery at the annual fair."

If they were sold as late as this it seems even odder that none has survived so we can know what they looked like. At least this version does fill in a few gaps, and since history, like life, is never simple, it is quite possible that two or three traditions flourished side by side.

What is beyond doubt is the association of *tawdry* with Saint Etheldreda and her fair. Words, like the times, almost always change for the worse, yet with such a handsome pedigree this one has come to a sad end. Indeed in Saint Audrey's own East Anglia it sank even lower, *tardry* being recorded in 1895 as meaning "shabby genteel, cheap finery," and also "immodest, loose, whorish". It is easy to see the connexion between cheap finery and cheap women. Somewhere I have read that Etheldreda herself is the patron saint of prostitutes; this I cannot confirm and it seems unlikely. There are plenty of penitent harlots in the calendar, why pick on a wife who refused even her husbands?

Nowadays if we bought a necklace we would expect it to be made of beads. *Bead* also is an unusual word, for instead of starting, as is common, by describing something concrete and immediate and widening its sense to include the metaphorical, it has gone the other way. In Chaucer's time a bead or *bede* was a prayer, from the Anglo-Saxon *gebed*, with a verb *biddan*, to pray. Thus to bid a bead is to offer a prayer, and beads bidding the saying of prayers. In the fourteenth century the two words sustained an uneasy co-existence: "With beodes and with prayers." Eventually, however, French *prière*, from Latin *precaria*, drove out the native *bede*.

Among the prayers said in churches was one that came to be known as the 'bidding prayer'. This was "a list of intercessions, read out after the Gospel at Mass," when prayers were asked "for the pope, prelates and clergy . . . for the realm and its prince, pregnant women, husbandmen, the harvest, the sick, pilgrims and benefactors, and lastly for the faithful departed . . . this was called bidding the Bedes," or praying the prayers. When 'this sense of the word *bid* went out of use, bidding prayer was thought to mean 'enjoining prayer', or issuing instructions about who and what should be prayed for. After the Reformation this practice disappeared, but has now been revived by the Roman Catholic Church. It seems a pity that they continue what the *OED* describes as "the vulgar error of calling this exhortation to the people the bidding prayer, as if it were a kind of prayer qualified by the attribute 'bidding'."

Beads were also told; that is, an account was kept of the number of times a particular prayer had been said. To *tell* once commonly meant to count or to reckon; now it survives in only a few fossilised forms—the *teller*, who pays out money or counts votes that have been cast, the *tally*, the *telling* remark and the phrase *all told*.

Telling beads is a practice older than Christianity; it entails using a number of seeds or similar objects strung on a cord as a device for keeping count of the prayers said. In the Roman Church this developed into what is known as the Rosary, traditionally invented by Saint Dominic, but common in various forms long before his time. Lady Godiva, who died about 1075, according to William of Malmesbury, "left by will to a certain statue of Our Lady 'the circlet of precious stones which she had threaded on a cord in order that by fingering them one after another she might count her prayers exactly'." The prayer usually said was the Our Father, hence, says Butler, "such articles were called *paternosters* and their makers . . . in London worked in Paternoster Row."

The Rosary finally became standardised as "a form of prayer or set of devotions consisting of the recitation or chanting of fifteen decades of Aves, each decade being preceded by a Paternoster and followed by a Gloria." The name comes from Latin *rosarium*, a rose garden, and seems at first to have implied a collection of devotions, flowers, as it were, presented to the Virgin. For what is known as the lesser rosary, five decades of Aves, is called a *chaplet*, explained by Brachet as follows: "The *chapelet de roses*, a chaplet of roses placed on the statues of the Virgin (shortly called a *rosaire* or rosary) came later to mean a sort of chain, intended for counting prayers, made of threaded beads, which at first were made to resemble the roses of the Madonna's chaplets."

These beads were either small, representing Aves, or large, representing Paternosters, and were 'told' by being passed through the fingers as each prayer was said. In time the prayer and the 'bead' that represented it became completely confused until at last 'prayer' was kept exclusively for the form of words and 'bead' for the "small globular perforated bodies" threaded on the string. By the seventeenth century beads were entirely secular, "used," says the *OED*, "as an ornament, either strung in a series to form a necklace, bracelet, etc., or sewn upon various fabrics." They might be of many materials; wood, glass, metal, jet or even amber, but never precious stones.

When in the fifteenth century sham gold and silver chains and faked jewels were known as Saint Martin's Beads it was a somewhat cynical pun. For the sanctuary of Saint Martin's le Grand, where criminals and rogues could take refuge from the law, was notorious as the haunt of men skilled at producing forgeries and passing them off as real. They became such a nuisance that Henry VI amended the Sanctuary Laws to forbid their being received there: "No workers of counterfeit cheynes, beades, broaches, ouches, rings, cups and spoons, silvered, should be suffered to remain therein." It was scarcely a respectable trade to be protected by the Church.

In the north of England, however, you might be lucky enough to have a set of beads made by Saint Cuthbert himself, for

On a rock of Lindisfarne
Saint Cuthbert sits, and toils to frame
The sea borne beads that bear his name.

"Although we do not learn," says Scott, that avid collector of legend, in a note to these lines, "that Cuthbert was during his life such an artificer . . . yet since his death he has acquired the reputation of forging those *Entrochi* which are found among the rocks of Holy Island, and pass there by the name of Saint Cuthbert's Beads. While at this task, he is supposed to sit during the night upon a certain rock, and use another as his anvil." Though the story told by "Whitby's fishers" is legendary, the Entrochi or Encrinites are not. Known as stone-lilies, they come from the jointed stalks of fossilised Crinoidea and are very common in limestone beds. Because of their beautiful shapes and regular size, and a fancied resemblance to a cross, they were often used as 'beads' by the country people.

Before the Reformation it was customary for those who could afford it to leave money for Masses to be said for the repose of their souls. Sometimes this charity took the form of the provision of houses where elderly men or women could live rent-free, their only duty being to pray for their benefactors. These, the original almshouses, were more generally known as *bedehouses* and those who lived in them as *bedeswomen* or *bedesmen*. The names of persons for whom remembrance was asked were entered on the *bede-roll*.

Nor did you need to be dead to keep a dependant to intercede for you. In Scotland there existed an 'order of paupers' honoured with the title of the King's Bedesmen, "to whom the Kings of Scotland were in the custom of distributing certain alms . . . and who were expected in return to pray for the royal welfare and that of the state." From the tragic history of the Stuarts it may be thought that they didn't get very good value for their money. Certainly in Scotland a beadsman came to mean a licensed beggar.

In Keats' *Eve of Saint Agnes*, however, with its conscious mediaeval trappings, the archetypal beadsman, lonely, cold and unregarded even in death, eternally prays:

> Numb were the Beadsman's fingers, while he told
> His rosary, and while his frosted breath
> Like pious incense from a censer old
> Seem'd taking flight for heaven, without a death.

Until at last, according to a cancelled version of the ending, after a thousand aves he 'stiffen'd', which seems hardly surprising, and was

> 'twixt a sigh and laugh
> Ta'en sudden from his beads by one weak little cough.

A beadhouse, or *bed-hus* in Anglo-Saxon, was sometimes called a *bed-aern*, a chapel or house of prayer. In some Yorkshire towns this word survives almost unaltered as a district or street called The Bedern; in York itself it was the residence of the Vicars Choral of the Minster. *Bed-hus* or *beadus* as it became in the north has disappeared, except in Welsh, where it was assimilated in the form *Bettws* and is found in many place-names—Bettws-y-Coed, Bettws-newydd, Bettws-Gwerful-Goch. It is a strange riddle and one to which we do not yet know the answer why Wales has so many bead-houses among her place-names and England none.

As with all living words, the meaning of *bead* can still be extended. When James Bond, gunning for Scaramanga, took out his Walther PPK "from under the pillow . . . and drew a quick bead on various objects round the room" he wasn't exactly praying for his soul but using part of the sighting apparatus.

Though it seems as if, in a secular way, beads may be coming back to their original purpose. For many a nervous man has been known to calm himself by running through his fingers a piece of knotted string. And America provides for the relief of tension a sort of miniature Rosary known as 'Worry Beads'.

4

FATHERS OF THE CHAPEL

Saint Martin of Tours was the son of pagan parents; his father, an officer in the Roman Army under Constantine, had destined him for a military career and even called him Martius or Martianus after the god of war. But Martin became a soldier much against his will, and did not care for the life.

He was still very young when, stationed at Amiens in northern France, one day, says Butler, "in a very hard winter, during a severe frost, he met at the gate of the city a poor man almost naked, begging alms of them that passed by. Martin, seeing those that went before take no notice of this miserable creature," wanted to help him, though "he had nothing but his arms and clothes. So drawing his sword, he cut his cloak into two pieces, gave one to the beggar and wrapped himself in the other half. Some of the bystanders laughed . . . but others were ashamed not to have relieved the poor man." And that night in his sleep Martin saw Christ "dressed in that half of the garment he had given away."

As a result of this vision Martin decided to abandon his military career for the religious life, and soon he was happily installed at an abbey near Poitiers. From there he had to be dragged, again protesting, to be consecrated Bishop of Tours, and here he remained till his death, much mourned by his people, about the year A.D. 400. He left behind, some say, his *capella* or little cloak, the very half, presumably, that he kept for himself; and this relic soon became the most treasured possession of the Frankish kings.

The Franks, who gave their name to France, were a race of

warriors. Under Charlemagne in the ninth century they occupied the whole of Western Europe, and the boundary of their empire is still represented by the division between the Germanic and Latin peoples. It is said they were impressive looking men, whose "fair or red hair was combed forward, leaving bare the napes of their necks." The royal family, however, as can be seen from the portrait on a seal of Childeric I, "were privileged to wear their hair long on their shoulders; if they were deposed their hair was cut, or more probably they were scalped."

A king, being in those days also the commander of the army, was constantly on the move. His money and valuables went with him in a chest, together with anything else too precious to leave behind. The *capella* most definitely came into this category. It was considered so holy that oaths were sworn on it as we swear them on the Gospels, and in a battle it was carried before the army to hearten the soldiers and bring them victory. Special guardians, called *capellani*, were appointed to ensure its safety, and quite naturally the name *capella* became transferred to the box or casket, probably richly jewelled, in which the cloak was kept. This reliquary, as it would now be described, had a place of honour in the palace during times of peace, and once again the name was extended, from the cloak to the box and from the box to the sanctuary in which it stood.

So great was the fame of Saint Martin's cloak that eventually all shrines where relics were preserved and all private sanctuaries were known as *capellae* or chapels, as the word became in English, from the French *chapelle*. A famous example is the magnificent *Sainte Chapelle* or Holy Chapel in Paris, designed by Saint Louis expressly to house the Crown of Thorns which he bought from the Venetian bankers to whom Baldwin of Byzantium had pawned it to get money to fight the Turks. Like a casket of rich sculpture and glittering glass, it was both a reliquary and a building where the King and his family could hear Mass.

Thus what we would call a chapel is a place of worship other than the parish or cathedral church; often a particular room set aside in a palace, embassy, prison, monastery, school and so on. In these chapels the services are conducted by a priest with special responsibilities for the institution concerned. He is the direct descendant of the old *capellani*, as his name shows, for he is a chaplain. Nowadays, however, he cares not for relics but for souls.

After the Reformation our parish churches passed to the established Church of England. Other denominations, not accepted as part of the establishment, had no 'church' to meet in. Their existence was tolerated rather than recognised; their places of worship were private and sometimes hidden, and spoken of indiscriminately as 'chapels'—that is, places where services not in accord with the rites of the Anglican Church were carried on.

If you had said in the seventeenth century you were going to 'Chapel' you would almost certainly have been going to Mass. Catharine of Braganza and other Catholic queens had their own chaplains and private chapels; so did the ambassadors from Catholic countries. "I have not," says Penn the Quaker in 1718, "look'd into any Chappel of the Roman Religion," and you can almost hear the horror in his voice. Boswell, on the other hand, was much drawn to Catholicism, and indeed became a convert for a short time in his youth. Visiting London in 1775, aged thirty-five, he is still tugged by the same invisible thread: "I intended to hear high mass in the Bavarian Minister's Chapel, but was too late . . . The Bavarian Chapel was the first where I heard the Romish service, with a wonderful enthusiasm; and therefore I love to go to it once while I am in London."

As time passed and Catholicism became less a crime than a political and social disability, public 'Romish chapels' began to appear. For safety's sake they were often referred to not by name, but by location; a London Catholic will still tell you he is going to Mass at 'Farm Street' or 'Maiden Lane'. Not till after the passing of the Catholic Emancipation Act were these chapels thought respectable enough to be recognised as churches.

Meanwhile the Dissenters were formulating their own ways of worship and gathering in the open air or in each other's houses in order to practise them. The Quakers, one of the earliest of these bodies to break away from the established Church, called their buildings 'meeting-houses', as indeed they still do. Other Nonconformists followed them in this, though John Wesley preferred to speak of 'preaching-houses'. Compare these names with the earlier *bed-hus* or 'praying-house', and you have an epitome of what each sect considered the most important element in religion.

By the nineteenth century, however, when the towns and villages of England were invaded by small plain brick buildings set up by the Methodists, the Baptists, the Congregationalists and others, they most of them bore the proud word 'Chapel', proclaiming their independence, over the door. 'Are you Church or Chapel?' used to be commonly asked when inquiring of a man's religion, and in the country at least Nonconformists are still indiscriminately lumped together as 'Chapel people'. But history is repeating itself, and we now quite naturally speak of a Methodist or Baptist church.

When Chapel appears in a place-name it is almost always one of the pre-Reformation kind. The best known, perhaps, is Chapel-en-le-Frith, 'the chapel in the woodland', a charming picture. In Kent and Surrey we even find the older form Capel surviving; as also in Capel Saint Andrew and Capel Saint Mary in Suffolk.

During its long life *chapel* has developed other and rather more bizarre connexions. It was, as the *OED* says primly, low or slang for "a privy or house of ease." Now a chapel of ease, according to the same authority, is "a chapel built for the convenience of parishioners who live far from the parish church." It is not hard to see how a parallel could be drawn with the little house at the bottom of the garden.

In Germany, however, chapel or *Kapelle* is the ordinary word not only for a church choir, but for an orchestra or band of any kind. The conductor is called the *Kapellmeister* or Master of the Chapel and this gives us the clue to the development in meaning. Germany before Bismarck had many princes and many courts; each prince had his private chapel, and he would appoint the best musican he could afford to pay to compose church music and take general charge of the playing and singing there. This was the position of *Kapellmeister*, and among those who held it in various courts were Handel, Haydn and of course Bach. When secular music was wanted the *Kapellmeister* would be expected to produce that too, and as the little courts fell slowly into decay the *Kapellmeister* with his *Kapelle*, that is his musicians and singers, began a new life as conductor and orchestra.

Then there is the strange connexion of chapels with the printing trade, entirely due to historical accident. When William Caxton returned to London from Bruges in 1476, bringing to England the newly invented process of printing, of which he had made himself a master, he looked about for somewhere to set up his press. The place he found was in the precincts of Westminster Abbey, part of the Almonry.

It might be thought that the monks, among the chief producers of books which they laboriously copied by hand, would have taken great interest in this new invention and have been its natural patrons. There is no suggestion, however, that room in the Abbey was in any way put at Caxton's disposal. The Almonry was the building from which alms, both in money and in kind, were distributed to the poor. Caxton appears to have had there a sort of lock-up shop, for which he paid ten shillings a year in rent. Other tenants had similar shops, and possibly the rent was a contribution towards the alms.

Caxton was printer, publisher, bookseller and sometimes translator all in one, and it was from here, under the sign of the Red Pale, that all his books were issued. *Pale* in this case is not that interesting word connected with *paling* and *beyond the pale*, but an heraldic term. The Red Pale, also employed by Caxton as his printer's mark, was a shield carrying down its centre a vertical stripe of red. Both this and the Almonry figure in the handbill he printed and distributed to advertise his *Ordinale Sarum*, said to be the first advertisement in the history of English publishing: "If it plese ony man spirituel or temporel to bye ony pyes of two and thre comemoracions of Salisburi use enpryntid after the forme of this present lettre whiche ben wel and truly correct, late hym come to Westmonester in to the Almonelrye at the Reed Pale and he shal have them good chepe."

This *pye* was a collection of rules governing the celebration of saints' days and greater and lesser feasts, indispensable to any priest saying Mass. It is the same word as the pie we eat; they both come from the Latin *pica* which is now used as the name of a kind of type. *Pica* really means a magpie, something black and white; how it acquired all these varied associations nobody really knows. Printer's pie, a mass of type all jumbled together indiscriminately or in confusion, may have got its name from the mixture of meat, herbs and spices that went into a mediaeval steak-and-kidney, or even from the *Ordinale Sarum* itself, the pages of which were so full of complications as to be practically unreadable.

There must have been something of an ecclesiastical atmosphere about Caxton's printing-shop, if only from the monks and friars and secular clergy who would drop in from time to time to inspect and wonder at the sheets coming off the press. Perhaps it became a private joke among his employees; certainly a verbal association with the Abbey clung to the trade and even now has not entirely disappeared.

For the workshop was referred to as a chapel, and this description soon came into general use. "Every Printing-House," says Home in 1688, "is termed a Chappel." The 'Chappel' included not only the building, but the men who worked there; later it extended to cover the whole ethos or 'mystery' of the craft of printing, rather in the fashion of the ancient guilds. There were, and indeed still are, orders, laws, secrets and customs of the Chapel. Its meetings discussed wages, prices, methods of work, conditions of apprenticeship and so on; its chairman was addressed, not perhaps without a sidelong glance at the ubiquitous priests, as the Father of the Chapel. It was, in fact, an early trade union, and as such it flourishes today. When there is a dispute in the printing trade you will hear of Chapels meeting to decide their policy, and whether or not to call the men out on strike.

Monks and friars also became part of printers' slang. The old presses, of course, had to be inked by hand; this was done with printers' balls, mushroom-shaped pads impregnated and then pressed over the type or forme to be printed. They worked quite well, except that it was difficult to ensure the ink was evenly distributed; sometimes there was too little or too much, or some letters might be missed entirely. What happened then was explained by Moxon in 1683: "Where the Pressman has not Destributed his Balls, some Splotches of Inck may be on them which he delivers upon the Form; so that the sheet printed on has a black Blotch on it: Which Blotch is called a Monk." The Black Monks were the Benedictines, and Westminster was a Benedictine Abbey.

Similarly, "when the Balls do not take, the untaking part of the Balls that touches the Form will be left White, or if the Pressmen skip over any part of the Form and touch it not with the Balls, though they do take, yet in both these cases the White place is called a Fryer." The White Friars were the Carmelites, distinguished by their white habits. Strangely enough, printing presses for long operated on the site of their priory, newspapers being published from Carmelite House. But modern type is mechanically inked by rollers instead of balls; monks and friars don't inhabit printing-houses any more.

Neither do the printers' devils, who once added an eschatological touch to the scene. These boys were employed to take the printed sheets off the press, and like all boys they soon got themselves covered with ink: "They do commonly so black and bedaub themselves that the workmen do jocosely call them devils." Though one early printer, the Venetian Aldo Manuzio, whose Aldine editions are collectors' items, was apparently accused in 1490 of employing a real devil in the person of a black slave. Somewhat tongue in cheek, he issued the following proclamation: "I, Aldo Manuzio, printer to the Doge, have this day made public exposure of the printer's devil. All who think he is not flesh and blood may come and pinch him." What the slave thought about such treatment isn't recorded.

All this is a long way from Saint Martin's little cloak. We do have another word for a private chapel which still survives, though with slightly Popish overtones—*oratory*. This too has an interesting history because of its connexion with *oratorio*.

Oratory is the Latin *oratorium*, from *orare*, to speak or to pray. It works both ways, an *oratio* being a prayer, men speaking to God, and an *oracle* the means by which he replied, God speaking to men. From *oratio* we get both *orison*, a prayer—"Nymph, in thy orisons be all my sins remembered"—and *oration*, a speech.

Now there was born in 1515 to a Florentine notary called Francesco Neri a son whom he christened Filippo. This boy was sent to live with relatives in Rome, and in that city he spent the rest of his life. He saw the sack of Rome by anti-Papal armies in

1527, and was so troubled by the wretchedness, disillusion and immorality of the post-invasion atmosphere he felt it his mission to bring back to these people the strength and comfort of the Church. In 1551 he was ordained priest, hearing confessions and talking to anyone who would listen, especially the young men, the teenagers of the time.

His headquarters was a small room or oratory built above the church of San Girolamo della Carità, and here he soon assembled a number of helpers, both clerical and lay. Before long the priests had acquired the title of Fathers of the Oratory or Oratorians, "because they rang a little bell to summon the faithful to prayers in their oratory." Saint Philip Neri lived to see his Congregation of "simple priests without vows, for plain preaching and popular services," approved by the Pope and spreading to other countries. Newman brought it to England; far more people have heard of Brompton Oratory than could say why it is called by that name.

An indispensable element of the "popular services" was music of all kinds. "On certain evenings of the week," says Grove, Saint Philip Neri's sermons "were preceded and followed either by a selection of . . . hymns or by a dramatic rendering of a scene from Scripture, adapted to the comprehension of an audience consisting chiefly of Roman youths of the humbler classes, the discourses being delivered between the acts of the drama." This idea was not really new; all drama began in the temples and the churches, though by the sixteenth century it had almost completely migrated to the secular stage. For Philip, however, nothing was alien that would interest the people and teach them to understand their religion. Everyone who could, helped; even Palestrina was persuaded to compose hymns and motets.

Soon these musical dramas, at first acted as well as sung though this practice was later dropped, became famous throughout much of Italy and far beyond. Evelyn, visiting Rome in 1644, "was invited to heare rare musique at the Chiesa Nova, a building of incomparable ordinance," to which the Oratorians had long since migrated. After the performance he judged it "the best Musick in the world . . . their motettos, which were sung by Eunuchs and other Voices, accompanied with Theorbas,[1] Harpsicors, & Viols; so as we were even ravish'd with the entertainment of that Evening." Subjects varied from the Judgment of Solomon, the Story of Abraham and Issac, and the Conception of the Blessed Virgin, to the Triumph of Chastity or lives of the saints—Catherine of Siena or, after his death, Philip Neri himself.

It is scarcely necessary to add that these performances were the original *oratorios*. Soon the word was internationally applied to such "extended musical compositions, usually of a sacred but not liturgical character, sung by solo voices and a chorus to the accompaniment of a full orchestra without the assistance of action, scenery or dress." We owe Saint Philip a great deal for popularising oratorios—the *Messiah*, maybe, the Bach *Passions*, and many other works down to Britten's *Saint Nicholas* and *Noye's Fludde*. Though I can't help feeling he might not entirely approve of the lack of provision for sermons in the intervals.

[1] large lutes.

5

BEGUINES AND BIGOTS

Beggar and *beg* sound such fundamental words we would expect them to be equally ancient as, say, work, eat and sleep. But this is not the case. It is true that, according to the *OED*, there was a rare Anglo-Saxon word *bedecian*—so rare it has been found only once, in the writings of King Alfred who, as kings went, was highly educated—and that this is "obscurely connected with Gothic *bidagwa*, beggar, from *bidjan*, to ask or beg." Even Alfred, however, could not drag it out of its obscurity. There is no trace of this or any similar form in English until we arrive in the thirteenth century and discover *beg* and *beggar* becoming firmly established.

These, it seems, came from quite a different stable. The idea has been put forward that the beggar was originally a *bagger*, getting his name from the bag he carried for scraps of food and other gifts he might receive. He would then be a relative of the *bag-man*, whom Brewer defines as "a commercial traveller, who carries a bag with samples to show to those whose custom he solicits. In former times commercial travellers used to ride a horse with saddle-bags sometimes so large as almost to conceal the rider." Nowadays, of course, they go by car. But this is another of those simple and apparently obvious etymologies which turn out to be without foundation. Our beggar had a different history; he almost certainly came in the first place from Liège in the Netherlands.

The twelfth century was a time of great ferment in the Church. Heresies were rife and often the zeal and enthusiasm of those who sought to suppress them seemed even more dangerous. Strange

48

sects and equally strange new religious and quasi-religious orders proliferated, some good, some bad. Things at times got just a little out of hand.

During the second half of this century (since the only date we have is that of his death in 1177) there lived in Liège a certain churchman called Lambert, nicknamed *le Bègue* or the stammerer. He has been described as a holy priest and a revivalist preacher; maybe he was both. It seems likely that, as with many of his cloth, he had a popular following of women, old and young, and that they must have asked him how best they could use their lives in the service of their religion. He proposed to found for them a new kind of lay or secular order, which did not entail taking vows or shutting themselves up in a convent, though they were expected to live in community and, of course, to be chaste. Just as the Benedictines, and later the Franciscans and Dominicans, took their names from their founders, so with Lambert's sisterhood. But for some strange reason he called them after his infirmity—Beguines.

Here, in the terse words of a contemporary annalist, is an account of how the order began: "God stirred up the spirit of a certain holy priest, a man of religion, who was called Lambert le Bègue (because he stammered) of Saint Christopher (in Liège), from whose surname women and girls who propose to live chastely are called Beguines, because he was the first to arise and preach to them by his word and example the reward of chastity."

The conditions of life in what became known as a Beguinage were pleasant and reasonable. The sisters "lived a semi-religious and somewhat austere common life without vows, but they were free to hold private property and to leave the community and marry." They were expected to occupy themselves with corporal works of mercy, "especially the service of the sick and needy, but they also devoted time to religious contemplation." Another account of them says that they professed "a life of poverty and self-denial, (and) went about in coarse clothing of undyed wool, reading the Scriptures and exhorting the people." This makes them sound much more like super-annuated Victorian governesses than they probably were. Such communities flourished for centuries in Germany, the Nether-lands, France and Italy, and a few of them, particularly in Belgium, still exist.

Though they wore no special habit, they did, it seems, wear a cap, which took its name from them and was known as a *beguin*, in English *biggin* or *biggonet*. This is described as a hood or coif, with flaps over the ears. It was worn in the sixteenth century by a serjeant-at-law. Something the same shape was often used for a night-cap. Shakespeare's Prince Hal, beside his dying father, compares the careful wakefulness of the king with the sweet sleep of him "whose brow with homely biggin bound Snores out the watch of night." It was also a child's cap, and thus sometimes used to symbolise the state of infancy: "How many dangers meet Poor man between the biggin and the winding sheet," wrote the poet Francis Quarles in 1638. It is quite possible the famous Biggin Hill in Kent may have been so called because of a fancied resemblance to this kind of coif or hood.

Often in the history of the Church male religious orders have been founded and women have later pressed to join them with some kind of modified rule. With the Beguines, however, events took the opposite course. The sisterhoods were so successful that men decided to set up parallel communities for them-selves.

These male brotherhoods were organised on similar lines to the Beguines, except that they kept a common purse and held no private property. This meant that unless they worked at a trade they had to support themselves by begging in the streets or from door to door, as the Franciscans and Dominicans, the

Mendicant Orders or Begging Friars, were by now already doing. At first they too took the name Lambert le Bègue had chosen, calling themselves Beguins. But in time, and for no clear reason, this appears in mediaeval Latin as *Begardus, Begardi*, or in common speech *Beghard*.

The Beghards seem to have caused dissension from the start of their career. It is said they were mainly weavers, dyers and fullers, the sort of militant trade unionists who during the Middle Ages were always making trouble for authority, whether Church or state. They had no particular discipline, often roamed about the countryside apparently answerable to no one, and were early suspected of being heretics. From the fourteenth century onwards "they were denounced by Popes and Councils and persecuted by the Inquisition"; by the seventeenth "such of them as still survived" were absorbed into the Third Order or Tertianii of the Franciscans.

Their stormy life was over, but they left their name behind. The Council of Trèves in 1370 had thundered against *laici, qui sub praetextio cujusdam religionis fictae Begardos se appellant . . . qui extra religionem approbatam validam mendicantes discurrent*—laymen, who under a false pretext of their religion call themselves Beghards . . . who without valid religious approval run about begging all over the place. It must have been a great opportunity for anyone tired of his job to take to the road, asking for charity in the name of Christ: *de begars et de begardes*, as a Frenchman wrote about the same time, *qui mengassent leur pain en oiseuse*— begards, male and female, who eat their bread in idleness. And this is the word, spelt in a fantastic variety of different ways, which established itself in English at the end of the fourteenth century as *beggare*, with its verb *beggen*, later to become beggar and beg. "Possibly", says the *OED*, "*beggen* was shortened from *beguiner* (to act the beguin), possibly (it was) taken (as a back-formation) from *beggare*, and this directly from Old French *begar* above." The history is complicated, but the outline is quite clear.

Wyclif was obviously using the word in its specific sense when he wrote disapprovingly of the Beghards, "newe sectis or ordris, bothe possessioners and beggaris, shulden ceese by Christis lawe," possessioners being those whose rule permitted them to hold land and property rather than relying on alms. In 1400 there is a description of "beggers with there hodes wide, With sleight and pale faces lene," which could pass for either meaning. But there is no doubt of Chaucer's intention when he tells us of his Friar that

> He knew the tavernes wel in every toun
> And everich hostiler and tappestere[1]
> Bet than a lazar or a beggestere.

The lazar we will come to later. As for the 'beggestere', in one respect the confusion of spelling remained for a considerable time. From its origin one might expect beg*gar* to be the proper spelling; in view of the large number of nouns in -er in English denoting someone who performs an action it is not surprising that by the fifteenth century the usual form was beg*ger*. So we have Queen Elizabeth's famous Act of 1597, "For the suppressing of Rogues, Vagabonds and Sturdy Beggers," under which, among others, the strolling players were liable to arrest and imprisonment. Why we have reverted in modern times to the more pedantic beg*gar* is not apparent. Johnson gives this form and the *Concise Oxford* recognises no alternative, either as a noun or a verb, though it does state that "a good beggar = begger, i.e., one good at collecting for charities, etc."

Another word that may be related to Beguine is *bigot*, originally meaning "a hypocritical professor of religion" and later "a person obstinately or unreasonably wedded to a parti-

[1] barmaid.

cular creed, opinion or ritual." It is an old word and has always been opprobrious; according to Wace in the twelfth century, "the French have much insulted the Normans, both with evil deeds and evil words, and often speak reproaches of them, and call them bigots and dreg-drinkers (*bigoz e draschiers*)."

Much play has been made with the resemblance to that favourite oath of Englishmen, By God! Partridge suggests that the sense of superstitious hypocrite "perhaps comes from the violent contrast between rough, uncivilised men's religious invocations and their crude behaviour." To Cotgrave in the seventeenth century the French *bigot* was "an old Norman word, signifying as much as *de par Dieu*, or for our God's sake," and meant "one that seems much more holy than he is." According to legend, as told by the *OED*, it originated "in the refusal of (the Norman) Hrolf or Rollo to kiss the foot of Charles the Simple, when, in the words of the twelfth century chronicler, '*lingua anglica* (! ! !) *respondit, Ne se, bi got, quod interpretatur, Ne, per Deum*'—he replied, in the English tongue, *Ne se, bi got*, which is interpreted, No, by God." Like all the best stories, however, this is "absurdly incongruous with the facts," though Bigod was certainly a Norman family name. It was borne by that Earl of Norfolk to whom Edward I, upon his refusal to fight in Gascony, remarked, "By God, sir earl, you will either go or hang!"; to which he pleasantly replied, "By God, sir king, I will neither go nor hang"—nor did he.

Whatever its origin, this term seems to have been confused, says Skeat, "with the word *beguin*, which was especially used of religious devotees." Ducange equates *Beguina* and *Begutta*, and in 1598 *bigin* and *bigot* are both defined as "superstitious hypocrite, or hypocritical woman." The fanatical behaviour and reputation of the Beghards would account for its later development.

The earliest recorded use of the verb to beg in 1225 is interesting, since it speaks of one who must "beggen ase on

E

harlot, yif neod is, his liveneth." Now the writers of the
Reformation, who always thought the worst of women and
particularly of women members of religious orders, had no doubt
about the morals of the Beguines. "This woorde 'Begyn' sholde
in his owne nature ryghtlye have ben expounded 'supersticious
or hipocriticall wemenne' ", says one. And another, even more
forthright, calls them "Young wanton wenches and beguins,
nuns and naughty packs.[1]" But strangely enough all this has no
connexion with our meaning of *harlot*, which originally belonged
to the rich and incredibly varied vocabulary our ancestors once
indulged in for describing rogues and beggars.

    This word *herlot, harlot, arlot*, has had an extraordinary number
of meanings. Primarily perhaps it signified a lad, a young
fellow, a 'knave', which has undergone a similar deterioration, a
person of low birth, a servant, a base fellow, a vagabond. It was
also early associated with impropriety, and in *Piers Plowman*
seems to refer to buffoons or tellers of ribald stories:

> Holde with none harlotes ne here nought her[2] tales . . .
> For it ben the deueles disoures I do the to understande,

where *disoure* corresponds to the modern French *diseur* or story-
teller. In Italian an harlot could be "a lack-Latin or hedge-
priest," or "a glutton, greedy-gut, great eater." It could even be
used in the sense of a good fellow; as Chaucer says of his
Somnour:

> He was a gentil harlot and a kinde;
> A bettre felawe sholde men nought finde.

And according to Skeat it comes from Old High German *heri*
or *hari*, an army, and the suffix—*lot*, with the sense of a loiterer;
hence "her-lot meant army loafer or camp follower." So if your
name is Arlott you may take your choice!

------

[1] useless baggages.   [2] their.

These meanings all agree in one respect, for though the word came later to be applied indiscriminately to both sexes, and eventually to women only, it started life as definitely masculine. This is a pity, since it rules out the rather charming explanation put forward by Lambarde in the sixteenth century that it derived from the name of Herleva or Arlette, the mother of William the Conqueror. William's father, Robert le Diable, Robert I, Duke of Normandy, riding through his Duchy, first saw her according to tradition, when she was dancing with the other village girls, or when she was kneeling by the water's edge washing her *bliauds*, which are said to be *vêtements de dessus que portaient au moyen ages les femmes et les hommes*. She was the daughter of Fulbert, a tanner of Falaise, and very beautiful:

> *Fille est d'un bourgeois la pucelle,*
> *Sage et courtoise et prude et belle,*
> *Et avait la couleur plus fine*
> *Que fleur de rose ni d'epine.*

Robert fell in love at sight and William was the result. And though his mother lived too soon to have to face jokes about being Arlette by name and *arlot* by nature, William himself only lost the title of 'the Bastard' by gaining that of 'the Conqueror'.

As for bastard, this derives from *bast*, the old French word for a pack-saddle. Men carrying their own or their master's goods in trains of horses or mules, corresponding perhaps to lorry-drivers today, would not expect a bed in the primitive wayside inns. Taking off their saddles, they would lay them on the floor and doss down on top of them. And if there were any accommodating women, well, they could always make room for two. So a *fils de bast*, with which they might be presented next time they came round, meant a pack-saddle child, got on the wrong side of the blanket, as opposed to a child of the marriage-bed; "a tersely allusive epithet for illegitimate offspring," as the *OED* puts it.

We have also a corresponding but less popular word *bantling*, more often used in English as an affectionate endearment for a child. This is a corruption of the German *Bänkling*, a child begotten on a bench or bank, and not in the marriage-bed.

6

THE CANTING CREW

"Thieves, beggars and gypsies," according to Captain Francis Grose, who compiled his *Classical Dictionary of the Vulgar Tongue* in the second half of the eighteenth century, went under the name of "The Canting Crew". And this strange word cant, says the *OED*, "presumably represents Latin *cantus, cantare*, singing, song, chant, French *chanter*, but details of its derivation and development are unknown."

The song or chant referred to is, of course, the church Latin of the monks and priests. *Cantare* is said to have been used contemptuously of such liturgical rites as early as 1185, when a certain Rigord, writing of another strange sect which had arisen in the Bourgres country, known as the Cotarelli, says that they led captive priests and religious, mockingly calling them *cantores*. They ill-treated them, giving them slaps (*dabant eis alapas*) or beating them with big sticks, crying *Cantate nobis, cantores, cantate*—sing to us, singers, sing!

It seems to have been the monotonous tone of the chant and the high key in which it was pitched that led to the adoption of the word to mean "a whining manner of speaking, especially of beggars." When the verb *to cant* first appeared in English in the sixteenth century it "applied to the tones and language of beggars, the 'canting crew': this, which according to Harman was introduced about 1540, may have come down from the religious mendicants; or the word may have actually been made from Latin or Romanic in the rogues' jargon of the time." It is unlikely though, I suppose, not impossible that it relates to the last syllable of *mendicant*.

The word *canting* or *cant*, then, signified "the speech and phraseology of Beggars", and especially 'the canting lingo', the secret language used by professional beggars, gipsies and thieves. In this sense it has been connected with the Irish and Gaelic *cainnt*, language, though it is probable the resemblance is no more than coincidental. William Harrison, in his *Description of England* prefixed to Holinshed's *Chronicle*, published in 1577, describes its origin thus: "Beggars, gypsies, etc . . . have dressed a language among themselves, which they name Canting, but others Pedlars French, a speache compact thirty years since of English, and a great number of odd words of their own devising, without all order or reason; and yet such it is, as none but themselves are able to understand. The first devisor thereof was hanged by the neck, as a just reward, no doubt, for his desartes, and a common end of all that profession."

Eric Partridge distinguishes three different streams of this river: "Note that Thieves' Latin is the jargon of thieves, Pedlar's French the jargon or cant not only of thieves but of other criminals and vagabonds, and Saint Giles' Greek the eighteenth century term for slang as distinct from cant." There is also gibberish or *gibbridge*, as it is sometimes written, which properly means "unintelligible speech, belonging to no known language." So Harsnet, writing of Roman Catholics in 1603, says, "They are agreed of certain uncouth non-significant terms which goe current among themselves as the Gipsies are of Gibridge, which none but themselves can spell without a pair of spectacles."

The origin of the word is unknown; *gibber*, meaning "to chatter like an ape" does not appear till later, yet *gibberish* would seem to stand for 'the language of gibber' as English is of England and Spanish of Spain. Grose indeed defines it as "the mystic language of Geber, used by chymists." Geber, a Europeanised form of the Arabic Jabir, is one of those all-inclusive names adopted by mediaeval scientists to give authority to their works. There may have been a certain Jabir ibn Hayyan, an alchemist of repute, living in the eighth century, but since more than two thousand books attributed to Jabir are known it is most unlikely that he wrote them all. Such was the power of the name, however, that a Spanish alchemist practising in the early fourteenth century chose to call himself Geber. Like many modern scientists, alchemists used a technical jargon quite incomprehensible to the uninitiated, which might well have been nicknamed 'Geberish'. But no support appears to be forthcoming for Grose's theory; most probably *gibber* is merely imitative of unintelligible speech.

Gibberish is also a secret method of communication rather than a tongue in its own right, "a sort of disguised language," as Grose explains, "formed by inserting any consonant between each syllable of an English word; in which case it is called the gibberish of the letter inserted: if F, it is the F gibberish; if G, the G gibberish; as in the sentence, How do you do? Howg dog youg dog?" This sort of thing can be endlessly varied, as all children know; Owho odo ouyo odo? was the one I used to use.

As a lover of words Partridge is fascinated by these secret languages, and so were many others before him. A certain Thomas Harman, 'Esquier', produced in 1567 "A Caveat for Common Cursitors, vulgarly called Vagabones, for the Utilitie and Proffyt of hys Natural Countrye". Cursitors, properly speaking, were "clerks of the Court of Chancery, whose office (abolished in 1835) it was to make out writs *de cursu*, i.e. of common official course or routine"—hence Cursitor Street in London, off Chancery Lane. They were also "Broken Pettyfogging attornies or Newgate solicitors", and even "low tramps or vagabonds".

When Grose published his highly entertaining *Dictionary* about two hundred years later he announced it was intended for

ordinary readers, "not only foreigners, but even natives resident
at a distance from the Metropolis, or who do not mix in the busy
world, (and who) without some help might hunt through all the
ordinary Dictionaries, from Alpha to Omega, in search of the
words 'black leg, lame duck, a plumb, malingeror, nip cheese,
darbies, and the new drop', although these are all terms of well-
known import at Newmarket, Exchange-Alley, the City, the
Parade, Wapping and Newgate." Nothing, they say, is more
ephemeral than slang, yet after another two centuries four at
least of these expressions are still in use—and how many of us
ever stop to think how they originated?

Apart from academic interest, such books in troubled times
might have a strictly practical value. Grose also quotes with
approval *English Villanies*, which appeared in 1638, proclaiming
itself to be "a booke to make gentlemen merry, citizens warie,
countrymen careful; fit for Justices to read over, because it is a
pilot by whom they may make strange discoveries"—much as it
was suggested that *Lady Chatterley* might have its educational
uses for the Establishment.

From this cant came to include any slightly arcane language
confined to a particular class or subject; what we would call
professional or technical jargon. Swift in 1727 inveighed against
such usage: "To introduce and multiply cant words is the most
ruinous corruption in any language." Had he lived today he
would have seen that statement proved true many times over.
And Sterne in *Tristram Shandy* asserted that "of all the cants
which are canted in this canting world, the cant of criticism is
the most tormenting."

Cant in its modern sense Gowers defines as "the insincere or
parrotlike appeal to principles, religious, moral, political, or
scientific, that the speaker does not believe in or act upon, or
does not understand." Such behaviour is always particularly
criticised in those who profess to hold strong religious views,

and so cant is also "affected or unreal use of religious or pietistic phraseology; language implying the pretended assumption of goodness or piety."

An interesting attempt was made in the *Spectator* of 1711 to derive this use of the word from "one Andrew Cant, who, they say, was a presbyterian Minister . . . who by exercise and use had obtained the Faculty, alias Gift, of talking in the pulpit in such a dialect that it's said he was understood by none but his own Congregation, and not by all of them." Andrew Cant, minister of Pitsligo in Aberdeenshire, and later in Aberdeen itself, lived from 1590 to 1663. His name, which is the same as that of Kant the philosopher, whose forebears were Scots, seems either to mean 'strong and lusty' or to be a shortened form of *cantor*, a singer in the church. From his history the former would seem to be the more appropriate.

Even if the dates fitted, which they do not, the *Spectator*'s derivation would be most unfair to Andrew, who sounds quite the opposite of a hypocrite. He had the reputation of being "ane super-excellent preacher", and having "once been a captain . . . was one of the most bold and resolute men of his day." Nor was his phraseology 'affected or unreal'. A strong Royalist, he once preached before a number of English officers in the time of Cromwell, and uttered such strong sentiments on duty to the King that "the officers rose up and some of them drew their swords and advanced towards the pulpit. The intrepid minister opened his breast and said, 'Here is the man who uttered these sentiments,' urging them to strike him if they dared." Yet his unfortunate name has associated him with vices he never seems to have possessed.

Of what we might call common cant, Johnson gave a witty if somewhat testy definition in one of his periodic outbursts to Boswell, who had professed himself "vexed" by the sad state of public affairs. On being pressed, he admits that "I did imagine I was vexed . . . but it *was*, perhaps, cant, for I own I neither ate less nor slept less." To which Johnson, crushingly, "My dear friend, clear your *mind* of cant. You may talk as other people do: you may say to a man, 'Sir, I am your most humble servant.' You are not his most humble servant. You may say, 'These are sad times; it is a melancholy thing to be reserved to such times.' You don't mind the times. You tell a man, 'I am sorry you had such bad weather the last day of your journey and were so much in the wet.' You don't care sixpence whether he was wet or dry. You may *talk* in this manner; it is a mode of talking in Society: but don't *think* foolishly."

Strangely enough *jargon*, which sounds so modern, is also a mediaeval word. It corresponds to Old French *gargon* or *gergen*, the warbling of birds, and once meant "the inarticulate utterance of birds or a vocal sound resembling it." The ald husband in Chaucer's Merchant's Tale. "was al coltissh ful of ragerye[1] And ful of Iargon as a flekked pye." It had the sense of unintelligible or meaningless talk or writing, gibberish, nonsense, as early as 1340:

> Swiche wordes of wise we wilnun to lere,[2]
> There nis no iargoun, no iangle, no iuggementis falce.

And *argot*, the French equivalent of cant, is another variant of jargon.

[1] wantonness.   [2] we wish to learn.

7

BEDLAM BEGGARS AND LAZARS

One among the many reasons why, in Elizabethan England, beggars and rogues swarmed everywhere like "maggots in a dead dog" was certainly the dissolution of the monasteries which, with their hospitals and charitable doles, had cared for many of the sick and poor. A few monastic hospitals, however, along with a few monastic schools, continued to survive; they were taken over by the state or by the Crown, becoming Royal Foundations. Among them was the famous Hospital of Saint Mary of Bethlehem in the City of London.

This building situated in Bishopsgate Without (that is, outside the city wall), on the north side of what was later to become Liverpool Street, was originally founded by Simon Fitz Mary, Sheriff of London, in 1247 as a priory "with the special duty of receiving and entertaining the Bishop of Saint Mary of Bethlehem and the canons and clergy of this, the mother-church, as often as they might come to England." Perhaps they did not come very often, for by 1330 the monks were also running a hospital for the sick and as early as 1402 they began, as we would say, to specialise in mental illness, housing "distracted people" and giving them what care they could. Perhaps because it had always been closely connected with the City of London, and under its protection and patronage, it escaped the heavy hand of Henry VIII. It passed into the control of the Mayor and citizens, and in 1547 was officially approved as a Royal Foundation for the reception of lunatics. "In this place," says Stow in 1603, "people that bee distraight in wits, are by the suite of their friends receyved and kept as afore, but not without charges to their bringers in."

Colloquially the hospital was known as 'Bethlehem', or in the more homely mediaeval spelling as 'Bedlam'. "He spak of a barne[1] In Bedlem, I you warne," says one of the Towneley Shepherds, meaning the city of David. So if a person were deranged he was fit for Bedlam; Clifford in *Henry VI* cries, "To Bedlam with him! Is the man grown mad?" Soon the word passed from the particular to the general, and was used for any lunatic asylum or madhouse—"Bedleme houses where madde and frantike men are kept"—or to describe whatever was mad or foolish, what Milton called "plain bedlam stuff".

Though they were housed and fed, there was little under-standing of how lunatics could be helped to regain their reason. "I stept into Bedlam," says Evelyn in 1657, "where I saw several poor miserable creatures in chains." Indeed in the seventeenth and eighteenth centuries Bedlam was one of the sights of London, a fashionable place to spend an hour on a Sunday afternoon: "Visitors went to Bethlem at Easter, Whitsun or Christmas, very much as the uncouth rustic goes to the menagerie of a travelling circus." *The World* in 1753 reports how a Londoner, to gratify the curiosity of a country friend, ac-companied him in Easter week to Bedlam; "to my great surprise I found there a hundred people at least who, having paid their twopence apiece, were suffered unattended to run rioting up and down the wards, making sport of the miserable inhabitants." It was, as Ned Ward, in *The London Spy*, remarked, "a hospital for the sick, a promenade of rogues, and a dry walk for the loiterers". This "indiscriminate admission of visitants" is said to have brought in a revenue of at least £400 a year. But there were always those who condemned the practice as inhuman and wrong, and it was finally forbidden in 1770.

[1] child.

Perhaps the best description was given by Thomas Brockbank, an aspirant to Holy Orders, visiting London fresh from Oxford in 1695: "We . . . walk'd to Bedlam, a delicate fine building but a most miserable spectacle within, for what can be more so than the sight of human shapes devoid of Reason. It consists of two very long Galleryes, that have abundance of little chambers, on one side; the first we came into is the place for men, where some are bound, some tumbling in straw, some talking without ceasing, some singing, etc: but this is nothing to what stir the women Kepe in an other Gallerye above this: there I met with such different sorts of Madness as one would not think human nature were subject to, some in deep sorrow, nothing but sighs and Tears, others in mad merriment, laughing aloud and even dancing again, some passing their time in trimming themselves tho nothing but raggs, others throwing off all their cloaths, and such a confus'd noise amongst them all as one cannot Imagine."

Without doubt Bedlam was "a scene of wild mad uproar" and confusion, "noisy, disorderly, haphazardly conducted, crazy". "Our house is a sort of Bedlam, and nothing in order," wrote a contributor to the *Guardian* in 1713. After several moves, to Moorfields in 1676 and to Lambeth in 1815, the Bethlem Royal Hospital still survives at Beckenham to care for the mentally sick. Here there is peace; it is in the world outside that bedlam has increased.

In spite of their treatment some poor souls did recover or partly recover. Those who were discharged and had no means of support "were licensed to beg, wearing as a badge a tin-plate on their left hand or arm"; they were known as bedlam beggars, bedlamers or bedlamites. Bethlehemites, however, were Christmas carol singers, according to Grose. Did they perhaps sing *Adeste fideles*—"Oh come ye, oh come ye, to Beth-lehem"?

Another name for bedlam beggars was Abram or Abraham

men; some think this comes from the Abraham Ward in Bedlam, "said to contain those lunatics who were, on certain days, allowed to go a'begging," others that it is an allusion to the parable in Luke 16, where "the beggar died, and was carried by angels into Abraham's bosom."

They might be mad or half-mad; more often they only pretended to be so. "To sham Abram" is given by Grose as a phrase especially current among sailors, "meaning to sham illness, to malinger." As for *malinger* itself, this clearly relates to the French *malingre*, sickly, of feeble constitution, scabby. Though there is no suggestion of pretended illness here, Weekley has unearthed an Old French form *malingreux*, which he says means "a beggar with artificial sores."

"An Abraham-man," explains an Elizabethan writer, "is he that walketh bare-armed and bare-legged, and fayneth hym self mad, and caryeth a packe of wool, or a stycke with baken on it, or such lyke toy, and nameth himself poore Tom." They made a practice of begging in lonely villages and at farmers' houses, "and if they espy small company therein they wyll with fierce countenance demaund some what."

In *King Lear* Edmund, Gloucester's bastard son, intriguing to replace his legitimate brother Edgar, conceals his double-dealing under "villanous melancholy, with a sigh like Tom o'Bedlam". And as if he had been given a cue, this is the disguise Edgar decides to adopt when he is driven out by his brother's treachery:

> . . . the basest and most poorest shape
> That ever penury, in contempt of man,
> Brought near to beast; my face I'll grime with filth,
> Blanket my loins, elf all my hair in knots,
> And with presented nakedness outface
> The winds and persecutions of the sky.
> The country gives me proof and precedent

Of Bedlam beggars, who with roaring voices
Strike in their numb'd and mortified bare arms
Pins, wooden pricks, nails, sprigs of rosemary;
And with this horrible object, from low farms . . .
Enforce their charity. Poor Turlygood! Poor Tom!

Another place well-known to beggars and criminals was Bridewell. Once a royal palace, it stood between Fleet Street and "the River of Themse"; here, according to Stow, "King Henrie the eight builded a stately and beautiful house of new, for receit of the Emperor Charles the 5 (nephew of Catharine of Aragon), who in the yeere of Christ 1522 was lodged himselfe at the blacke Friers but his Nobles in this new builded Bridewell, a Gallery being made out of the house over the water . . . into the Emperors lodging." Its name of Bridewell came from a nearby holy spring or well called Saint Bride's or Saint Bridget's Well. Saint Bride's Church, rebuilt after the Great Fire, still stands in the neighbourhood.

Though "King Henrie himselfe often times lodged there also," he seems to have tired of the place; perhaps because "in 1529 the same king Henrie and Queene Katherine were lodged there, whilst the question of their marriage was argued in the Blacke Friers," that is, by the Papal legates. From 1531 it was occupied by the French Ambassador as his official residence, but shortly before his death in 1553 Edward VI decided to present it to the City authorities. "Sir George Barne, being Maior of this Citie," records Stow, "was sent for to the Court at White Hall and . . . the king gave unto him for the Comminaltie and Citizens to be a Workehouse for the poore and idle persons of the Citie, his house of Bridewell and 700 Markes land . . . and all the bedding and other furniture of the . . . Hospitall of the Savoy." And before long it had been converted again, this time into what was known as a 'House of Correction', "a building for the confinement and punishment of offenders, especially with a view to their reformation."

The setting up of such institutions was provided for by a Statute of Queen Elizabeth in 1575: "In everye Countye . . . one Two or more Abyding Howses . . . shalbe provided, and called the Howse or Howses of Correction for setting on worcke and punishinge . . . of such as shalbee taken as Roges." To go to a House of Correction was the equivalent of being sentenced to hard labour. Gaols as such were not intended as places where criminals could be lodged indefinitely; they were sent there to be "kept in safe custody pending their trial, their execution, their transportation or the payment of their debts." Dissolute paupers, idle apprentices and women off the streets were the kind of people for whom Houses of Correction were intended, and an Act of George II urged justices to "take effectual care that (they) . . . be duly fitted up, furnished and supplied with sufficient implements, materials and furniture for keeping, relieveing, setting to work, employing and correcting all idle and disorderly persons, rogues, vagabonds, etc." From the chance location of the London house these institutions were generally known as bridewells throughout the country.

Pepys visited "New Bridewell" in 1664 and thought it "very handsome. Several at work, among others one pretty whore brought in last night, which works very lazily. I did give them 6d to drink, and so away." On another occasion he was feeling more generous, but then he was being shown the accompanying workhouse where the Bridewell boys were charitably maintained: "The clerk did lead me up and down through all the house, and there I did with great pleasure see . . . the little children employed, everyone to do something, which was a fine sight, and worthy encouragement. I cast away a crowne among them."

The conditions in the London Bridewell, which appears to have been somewhat better than those in the provinces, were re-

ported on in 1777 by that intrepid philanthropist John Howard, who had been driven by a short experience of captivity in France to devote his life to studying the state of prisons, and improving the treatment and relieving the sufferings of the prisoners. There were two wards, he says, one for men and one for women, each consisting of a day-room "in which they beat hemp", and a night-room where they slept. The prisoners were kept within doors and never allowed any exercise in the fresh air, "which makes it necessary to limewhite the rooms twice a year." There was an infirmary but, as Howard laconically remarks, "no bath". In winter the women had "some firing" and the night-rooms were "supplied with rye-straw once a month. No other prison in London has any straw or bedding."

The prisoners worked in winter from eight to four, in summer from six to six, excluding meal-times. Howard found them always busy; "at my last visit they were picking oakum." Their employer was "a hemp-dresser, who has the profit of their labour, an apartment in the prison and a salary of £20." The workers got precisely nothing. A steward provided their meals, for which he was allowed eightpence per day per prisoner. Out of this he supplied "on Sunday, Monday, Tuesday and Thursday a penny loaf, ten ounces of dressed beef without bone, broth and three pints of ten shilling beer: on Wednesday, Friday and Saturday a penny loaf, four ounces of cheese or some butter, a pint of milk-pottage, and three pints of beer." Howard, however, disapproved of the beer and even more of the fact that if prisoners could get money they could always buy extra intoxicants, most probably at exorbitant prices. He thought no liquor should be served in prisons "except milk, whey, buttermilk or water . . . How many persons have I known . . . who have gone into prison sober men; but who have either destroyed themselves there by drinking, or have gone out mere sots?"

The idea of bridewells, where those who had gone astray

F

might be "corrected by diligence and labour", was a good one, and it must have induced in many "idle apprentices" a healthy fear of what the dramatist Killigrew called "Bridewell hemp, brown bread and whipcord." But as prisons were reformed and understanding grew, the name, together with the institution, vanished. Though dictionaries continue to list the word, its relevance has become purely historical.

Another word that owing to time and circumstance has dropped out of use is *lazar*, a shortening of the proper name *Lazarus*, in which form it was once applied to beggars, and more particularly to those both poor and diseased: "Lazares ful monye, summe lepre, summe lome and lomerande[1] blynde." Its origin is the parable already quoted, about "a certain rich man, which was clothed in purple and fine linen, and fared sumptuously every day: and . . . a certain beggar named Lazarus, which was laid at his gate, full of sores and desiring to be fed with the crumbs which fell from the rich man's table: moreover the dogs came and licked his sores."

As far as I know, Lazarus is the only character in all his stories to whom Christ gave a definite name; it would be interesting to know why. Possibly because this parable may have been based on an old Egyptian folk-tale current in Palestine, possibly even to drive home the lesson that "they will not be persuaded, though one rose from the dead," by contrast with the other Lazarus who proved the saying to be true. Lazarus is the Greek form of the Hebrew Eleazar, meaning 'God helped' or 'God will help'. As a Christian name it has never been popular in England; this is not surprising when as late as the eighteenth century Johnson was defining *lazar* as "one deformed and nauseous with filthy and pestilential diseases".

In the Neapolitan dialect the word continued to keep its uncomplicated sense of beggar or rogue, the two being in the

[1] stumbling.

minds of most men synonymous; the famous or infamous *lazzaroni* of Naples are beggars to this day, so called, says Brewer, "from the hospital of Saint Lazarus, which served as a refuge for the destitute." Elsewhere, however, it narrowed down to describe a sufferer from one of the most widespread and, after the plague, most feared diseases of the Middle Ages, leprosy. As Holland said in 1610, "Lazars—so they used to tearme folk infected with the Elephantiasie or Leprosie." And Caxton speaks of a man to whom "God sente . . . suche a sekeness that he became lazare and mesell." This *mesell* was another word for leprous, from the Latin *misellus*, a diminutive of *miser*, wretched, though it later became confused with measles, referring to spots or blisters on the skin. *Leprous* itself is the Latin *lepra*, scaly, from Greek *lepos*, a scale, a white and scaly condition of the flesh being one of the characteristics of leprosy.

Very early lepers were shunned by their fellow men and required to advertise their presence so that others could keep out of their way. "They provided for the lazer," says Holinshed, "to keepe him out of the city from clapping of dishes and ringing of bells." No one would give them work and they were forced to live on charity. This produced at the end of the last century a brilliant flight of fancy from a certain Mr Jephson, who maintained that "rope-making was one of the few occupations permitted to lepers, and that rope-walks were often attached to their dwellings, so the trade remained long obnoxious in consequence." According to his theory the name *lizard*, apparently a corruption of *lazar* or *lazarus*, "is in many instances still applied to the old part of towns where a rope-walk is situated," and finding one in the neighbourhood of the Lizard Point in Cornwall, and of Lezardrieux in Brittany, he proposes this explanation of the origin of that name. Unfortunately he doesn't seem to have taken into account the fact that the language common to Cornwall and Brittany was Celtic, not Anglo-Norman with cosmopolitan additions. The Lizard gets its name, so the authorities say, not from any connexion with lazar or any fanciful resemblance of the shape of the Point to a reptile, but from two Cornish words *lis*, a hall, and *ard*, high. Once a high hall stood there, and presumably another stood at Lezardrieux.

In time monks and friars, and also the secular authorities, busied themselves with caring for these outcasts. Hospitals were set up where they could be looked after and where they could also be isolated to prevent their handing on the infection. Such a hospital was known at various times as a lazar-cote, lazar-house, lazaret or lazaretto. Biddulph, travelling in Greece in 1609, speaks of "the Lazaretto (at Zante) which is a place like unto the pesthouse in Morefields", the pest being the plague or any other fatal epidemic. But by the time an Act was passed in 1800 for "erecting a lazaret on Chetney Hill, in the County of Kent", its purpose had become rather different, since there is a further provision "for reducing into one Act the laws relating to Quarantine."

As early as 1605 *lazaretto* is used with the meaning of "a building, sometimes a ship, set apart for the purposes of quarantine." The reference is to Ben Jonson; "where they used to lie out forty, fifty dayes, sometimes, about the Lazaretto, for their triall." Of course if it is *quarantine* it should properly be forty days, from the Italian *quaranta*, forty, *quarantina*, a set of forty, as we might say two score. A word *quarantain*, with this meaning, was introduced into English but failed to establish itself. Fashion in words is as fickle and inexplicable as in any other sphere; we quite happily talk of a *fortnight* (fourteen nights), but the corresponding *sennight* (seven nights) long ago disappeared in favour of *week*.

Originally quarantine seems to have been connected with *Quarentena*, the mediaeval Latin name for the desert or wilderness into which Christ was "led up of the spirit . . . to be tempted of the devil. And when he had fasted forty days and forty nights, he was afterward an hungred." One would have expected, therefore, that quarantine would be the name for Lent, but history developed rather differently. In its commonest use it was an ancient legal form, signifying "a period, originally of forty days, during which a widow, entitled to dower, had the right to remain in the chief mansion-house of her deceased husband." *Dower*, cognate with *dowry* and *endow*, is "that portion of property to which, on her husband's death, the widow is entitled for the maintenance of herself and children—one-third and upwards of the estate for life." Hence the existence of dower houses in which such widows lived, and their title of *dowager*.

Forty has always been, like seven, a mystic number, a good figure to pick on if you need something fairly large. This, rather than any logical medical reason, probably led to its adoption for the period of isolation we now know as quarantine, "a period," as defined by the *OED*, "originally of forty days, during which persons who might serve to spread a contagious disease are kept isolated from the rest of the community." According to A. C. Crombie, it was at Venice and at the related port of Ragusa (now Dubrovnik) that such regulations were first made. Both had much trade with the east, and the "merchant-ships built at or sailing from Ragusa," the *ragusea nave* or "Aragousey shippes", have given us our word *argosy*, meaning a large merchant vessel. In 1377 Ragusa issued a law "ordering the isolation of all travellers from infected regions for thirty days (called the *trentina*), and Marseilles in 1383 extended their period to forty days . . . thus instituting the quarantine." Though Ben Jonson mentions the practice, the actual word seems to have been first used in English by Pepys in 1663.

This period of enforced isolation may account for our English habit of sending people to Coventry or, as the *OED* puts it, of excluding a man "from the society of which he is a member on account of objectionable conduct." Grose describes this as a military term and explains it thus: "(An officer) sent to Coventry is considered as absent; no one must speak to or answer any question he asks, except relative to duty, under penalty of being sent to the same place. On proper submission, the penitent is recalled; and welcomed by the mess, as just returned from a journey to Coventry." This is well illustrated by a Hunt Book entry of 1765 which records how a Mr John Barry, having contrived to get the hounds in the wrong place at the wrong time, "was sent to Coventry, but returned upon giving six bottles of Claret to the Hunt."

The origin of the phrase has never been explained. The quotation usually given is from Clarendon's *History of the Rebellion* of 1647: "At Bromingham, a town so generally wicked that it had risen upon small parties of the king's, and killed or taken them prisoners and sent them to Coventry (then strongly held for the Parliament)." Brewer has a tale "that the citizens of Coventry had at one time so great a dislike of soldiers that a woman seen speaking to one was instantly tabooed; hence when a soldier was sent to Coventry he was cut off from all social intercourse."

Either of these would tie up with Captain Grose's suggestion that this is army slang, though nowadays it is more often applied to workers who have broken some written or unwritten Trade Union rule. But Logan Pearsall Smith thinks that *Coventry* is no more than a popular corruption of *quarantine*. It could be so.

8

THE BEARDED LADY

Among the treasures of Westminster Abbey is a stone statue, about half life-size, crowned and robed in a flowing gown, with a handsome if somewhat worn face and a luxuriant beard and moustache. An Anglo-Saxon saint, you might think, and you wouldn't be far wrong. Only when you notice something a little odd about the figure do you realise this is not a he-saint at all, but a she-saint with a large quantity of superfluous hair. Who was she and how did she get that way?

Tradition says she was called Wilgefortis, though she was more generally known throughout Western Europe, for reasons which will appear, by an affectionate nickname varying from country to country, but always with the same sense. Uncumber, they called her in England—holy Saint Uncumber.

She seems to have been born, again according to tradition, in the era of once upon a time, when Portugal was still ruled by a heathen king, either Moslem or barbarian. His wife, who was probably Christian, presented him one day with seven, or some say nine, children at one birth. The whole litter miraculously lived and thrived and grew up to become Christian in their turn. All of them eventually suffered martyrdom; what happened to the mother the story does not say.

Among these sturdy children was Wilgefortis. Her father, following the usual policy of kings, arranged a dynastic marriage for her with the king of Sicily. However, she did not wish to marry, and this she explained to her father. With her mother's example in mind, her objection seems scarcely surprising. The reason she gave was conventional and popular, though none the

75

less sincere; as a Christian she had made a vow of virginity, which she did not intend to break.

The king, as kings do, brushed her inclinations aside; the wedding must go on. So Wilgefortis' only resource was to pray in her distress for help from heaven. It came in the shape of a long drooping moustache and a silky curling beard, making her look like a sort of female Viking, except that she was probably dark. Here the king showed himself either as an honest man or as lacking in political expediency, for instead of arranging for her to hide her face under a veil, he seems to have allowed the king of Sicily to see her, whereupon he refused to have anything to do with such a freak. After all, the affliction might be hereditary; who would want seven (or nine) daughters, all with beards? This was more than poor Wilgefortis' father could support, and in a fit of rage he had her crucified.

Fashions change. There aren't many women these days who would prefer a beard to a husband. Nor are the men quite so easily put off—not if the Bearded Lady in Auden's libretto for *The Rake's Progress* is any precedent. Then there is Evelyn Waugh. I can't help wondering whether, when he created Clara in *Love Among the Ruins*, he might have had the story of Saint Wilgefortis in mind, and gently turned it upside down, along with much else in his entirely rational world where the Government's busiest department offers quick and clean euthanasia to those who are tired of life.

Clara, the ballet dancer, afraid of losing her figure, is sterilised, but the operation goes wrong. As a result she develops "a long, silken, corn-gold beard". Miles Plastic, the modern man, is utterly fascinated. "Her smile started in her wide grey eyes. Her lips under her golden moustachios were unpainted, tactile. A line of pale down sprang below them and ran through the centre of the chin, spreading and thickening and growing richer in colour till it met the full flow of the whiskers, but leaving on either side, clear and tender, two symmetrical zones, naked and provocative . . . 'I think your beard is beautiful,' he said." After an idyllic love-affair Clara finds she is pregnant. Preferring ballet to babies, she undergoes a second operation, losing both the baby and the beard, which is replaced by "a wonderful new substance, a sort of synthetic rubber that takes grease-paint perfectly." This is too much for Miles. Appalled, he can say only, "I think I shall go for a short walk." He does and never sees her again.

One tale sounds scarcely less fantastic than the other; they might both be equally true. Nowadays, however, we like our saints to be historical and Butler's *Lives* says of Wilgefortis, "Her story is a curiosity of hagiology . . . it has the unenviable distinction of being one of the most obviously false and preposterous of the pseudo-pious romances by which simple Christians have been deceived or regaled." With respect, this seems to me a little hard. Wilgefortis is no worse than Cinderella, and filled as clear a need. It was the 'simple Christians' who invented her, and they got a lot of fun out of doing it. But why does she feature in a book about words? Because of her name, because of her nickname, because she has been almost explained away as a misunderstanding of a statue and a word. Almost but not quite, since for centuries she existed in the minds of men and in the minds of women with even firmer conviction.

It was Father Charles Cahier, S.J., who wrote, "For my part I am inclined to think that the gown, beard, crown and cross which are regarded as the attributes of this marvellous maiden are only a pious devotion to the famous crucifix of Lucca, somewhat gone astray." This crucifix, the *Volto Santo* or Holy Face, once believed to be a likeness of Christ carved by Nicodemus himself, was much venerated and an object of pilgrimage. As with many other statues, the figure was displayed in rich clothes and wearing a jewelled crown. The long robe, according to Father Cahier, "caused it to be thought that the figure was that of a woman, who on account of the beard was called *Vierge-forte*." A *femme forte* is a stout woman, *liqueurs fortes* are strong drink; by analogy, then, *vierge forte* is a strong, stout, doughty virgin, and this could easily corrupt to Wilgefortis. Another suggestion is that the name might come from *Hilge vartz*, holy face.

This explaining away of Wilgefortis sounds plausible and fascinating. I am not scholar enough to go into its implications, and yet there are one or two points that leave me slightly unsatisfied. After all, it was common practice in the Church, and is still common practice in many Catholic countries, to dress images of the Virgin and the saints in embroidered robes and golden crowns. Other crucifixes besides the one at Lucca were similarly adorned, yet this does not seem to have led to a general heresy that Christ was a bearded woman. And some classes of men, to say nothing of priests and monks, wore long robes at least till the seventeenth century. It is strange too, if the *Volto Santo* was the origin of her cult, that she should emerge with a French or Germanic name and be located in Portugal. The *Hilge vartz* derivation certainly appears the more likely, since the title Holy Face given to this particular crucifix was specific and possibly unique. But the legend about its coming to Lucca is very strong and very old; the Christians who invented another story about it must have been not only simple, but downright ignorant. Indeed it is nowadays recognised as a scientific fact that the chromosome make-up of an apparent woman might cause the development at puberty of such male secondary sexual characteristics as the growth of a beard. Girls were married very young in those days, and so it is possible the 'miracle' may even have actually happened.

It was not, however, for her beard or her crucifixion that the people loved her. They remembered that when she asked for help from heaven the help came, even if in a somewhat questionable shape. Because of this they turned to her when they were in trouble, believing she would free them from their worries and ensure for them a happy death. Thus she acquired the additional name of *Liberata*, the deliverer, with its many variations; *Livrade* in France, *Ontkommer*, *Kümmernis* in Germany, *Regenfledis* in Flanders, and in England, delightfully, Uncumber.

Cumber, possibly the same as German *kummer*, trouble, is not much used nowadays. We wouldn't speak of Martha being "cumbered about with much serving," or of a useless thing or person as a cumber-ground, though we might say it was cumbersome. Originally it meant to harass, distress or trouble, and thus to uncumber was to remove the trouble or harassment. Now we use encumber, meaning to hamper, hinder or burden, with disencumber as its clumsy opposite. If we still prayed to Liberata I suppose we should address her as Saint Disencumber.

Uncumber should, perhaps, be the patron saint of the Divorce Courts, if this were possible. English women in particular, reversing the idea that the wife is the 'trouble and strife', tended to regard their husbands as the trouble from which they longed to be delivered. Less wise than Wilgefortis, they got themselves married and then wished they hadn't, or more probably wished they were married to a more attractive man. Forbidden divorce, they had no way of getting rid of their husbands short of murder or an act of God. This, they felt sure, she would graciously understand, and they prayed to her and brought her offerings "to uncumber them of their husbands."

The final bizarre touch to this story is that the offering commonly consisted of a bag or a sheaf of oats. "She seems," says Ivor Brown, "to have had a curious and somewhat farmyard appetite, since the usual offering made by distressed wives in search of conjugal relief was a gift of grain. Of Saint Uncumber Sir Thomas More observed that 'for a peck of oats she would provide a horse for an evil husband to ride to the devil upon.'"

But why oats? Nobody seems to know. Nothing in the legend of Wilgefortis accounts for it, and the practice is a typically pagan one.

There is, however, an odd connexion between the name Liberata and the food of horses, which is interesting though I would not claim it to be more than fortuitous. In the days when men kept horses as we keep cars, as an essential means of transport, there were many people who had, as it were, no garage space. Instead of stabling the horse in their own back-yard they might, especially if they lived in a town, board it out 'at livery', in the care of a livery-stable keeper. Such a man was Thomas Keats, the father of John; head ostler in the Swan and Hoop Livery Stables at Finsbury Pavement, he married his master's daughter and succeeded to the business. Here in this horsey atmosphere Keats lived as a child, until his father was killed by a fall as he rode home one Sunday "at a late hour", having dined, perhaps too well, with friends in Southgate.

And what was this livery? Another poet, Edmund Spenser, explained it clearly and tersely in 1596: "What livery is, we by common use in England know well enough, namely that it is allowance of horse-meat, as they commonly use the word in stabling; as, to keep horses at livery; the which word, I guess, is derived of livering, or delivering forth their nightly food. So in great houses, the livery is said to be served up for all night, that is, their evening allowance for drink; and livery is also called the upper weed which a serving-man wears; so called, as I suppose, for that it was delivered and taken from him at pleasure."

By horse-meat, of course, he does not mean as we would the carcase that goes to the horse-butcher. He is using the word in its old sense of food of any kind, as we still do when we say that one man's meat is another man's poison. Horse-meat is "the pro-vender of horses"; Phillips in 1706 defined "Livery of Hay and

Oats" as "the giving out of a certain quantity for feeding horses." And this is where we are back with Saint Liberata who "for a peck of oats . . . would not fail to uncumber (women) of their husbands." For livery comes from the French *liveré*, the old form of *livré*, past participle of the verb *livrer*, to deliver. And this, of course, comes ultimately from the Latin *liberare*, as does Liberata itself. So a livery of oats was delivered to the deliverer to encourage her, as we might say, to deliver the goods.

There is another saint, introduced to me by Douglas Woodruff, who shares with Uncumber the distinction of having "achieved canonisation although he never existed, which is a much greater handicap to sanctity than being born in original sin"—Saint Expeditus. He is said to have been a soldier in the Roman army, and martyred at Melitine in Armenia in the fourth century, but the only evidence for his existence is the mention of his name in an ancient Martyrology "among a group of martyrs both on the 18 and 19 April." And, adds Butler, "there is no vestige of any tradition which would corroborate either mention, whereas there is much to suggest that in both lists . . . the name is merely a copyist's blunder."

A story purporting to account for the gentleman's name was told of some French nuns in the nineteenth century. A packing case containing relics from the catacombs of Rome was sent to their convent in Paris; on the label was written *Spedito*, i.e., sent off, and the date of dispatch. But the nuns "mistook this for the name of the martyr and set to work with great energy to propagate his cult." This tale, however, is probably *ben trovato* rather than true, since Butler points out, "as far back as 1787 . . . Saint Expeditus was chosen patron of the town of Acireale in Sicily," and a popular cultus of the saint was in existence in Germany in the eighteenth century, where he was "invoked against procrastination."

Quite naturally so, with a name like Expeditus. Though

hagiographers deplore the fact, "some good people were led to believe that, when there was need of haste, an undertaking committed to his patronage was likely to meet with prompt settlement," and this "*calembour* or play upon words" has led to what Father Delehaye calls "his surprising and regrettable popularity . . . as the advocate of urgent causes." *Calembour*, by the way, means a pun or jest; it comes from "Wigand von Theben, a priest of Kahlenberg in Lower Austria," a character in *Til Eulenspiegel* and other German tales. He was "noted for his jests, puns and witticisms," and in French translations of the stories appears as the Abbé de Calembour.

Expeditus, of course, from Latin *expedire*, is the same as our expedite, "to free from difficulties, to help forward, to dispatch, send off." It comes from *ex*, out, and *pes*, *pedis*, foot, and meant literally "to free a person's feet from fetters, to extricate the foot," the opposite of *impedire* or impede, "to put someone's feet in shackles, hence to hinder, obstruct." Indeed it might even be that this 'saint' came by his name from the note of a scribe that a prisoner was freed of his fetters—*expeditus*.

9

TO BE YOUR VALENTINE

"It was Saint Valentine's Day. Februato Juno, dispossessed, had taken a shrewish revenge on that steadfast clergyman, bludgeoned and beheaded seventeen centuries back, and set him the ignominious role of patron to killers and facetious lovers. Guy honoured him for the mischance and whenever possible went to mass on his feast-day."

So Evelyn Waugh of his hero, Guy Crouchback, in *Men at Arms*. Nor can he have been the first to sympathise with Saint Valentine in his misfortune, since whatever we commemorate or used to commemorate on February 14 certainly has nothing whatever to do with the martyr or martyrs whose feast-day it is.

There are at least two Saints Valentine or Valentinus, with remarkably similar stories. Butler says, "Valentine was a holy priest in Rome, who . . . assisted the martyrs in the persecution under Claudius the Goth. He was apprehended and sent by the emperor to the prefect of Rome who, on finding all his promises to make him renounce his faith ineffectual, commanded him to be beaten with clubs, and afterwards to be beheaded, which was executed on February 14, about the year 270." The Roman Martyrology also includes a second saint, the Bishop of Interamna or Terni, who suffered on the same date and in the same manner, both executions taking place on the Flaminian Way. This does not, however, discount the story; "though the surviving accounts of both martyrdoms are clearly legendary," maintains the *Oxford Dictionary of the Christian Church*, "there are indications that each contains a nucleus of fact; and it is just possible that the kernel of truth in the two legends refers to a single person."

Certainly the name Valentinus has always been quite popular, though never widespread, and appears in England from the twelfth century onwards, used indiscriminately for men and women. It derives from the Latin *valens*, meaning strong and healthy, *vale*, the Roman parting salutation, being quite literally translated into English as *fare well*, may things go well with you. *Welfare*, of course, is the state of faring well; our *goodbye* has quite a different origin, having been contracted from the longer *God be with you*, or *God be wi' ye*.

Some Roman Valentinus probably gave his name to the city and province of Valencia in Spain, and also to the district of Valence in France. Cesare Borgia at an early age was made, by his father the Pope, Cardinal of Valencia; because of this he was known to the Italians as *Il Valentino*. When he renounced the purple and married Charlotte d'Albret, sister of the king of Navarre, Louis XII conferred on him the French Duchy of Valentinois, so he kept the same title to the end of his life. Valentino to a modern reader, however, is more likely to mean the great lover of the silent screen, one of the first film stars to become a legend long before his death.

The surname de Valence, later spelt Valance, Vallans or Vallins, is said to have come to England with the half-brothers of Henry III, the Earls of Pembroke. It was the widow of Aymer de Valence, Earl of Pembroke,

> . . . sad Chatillon, on her bridal morn
> That wept her bleeding love,

who founded Pembroke College, Cambridge, about 1347. Unfortunately, however, Pembroke was not, as tradition says, "slain at a tilting match held in honour of her nuptials," but died suddenly in France a matter of three years later.

As for the "fringe of drapery, now applied to part of the bed hangings," and known as a *valance*, the *OED* will not allow

any connexion here with Valentine. The origin, it says, is obscure, though it may be connected with French *avaler*, to descend, and thus presumably to hang down, as in *avalanche*, a *val* being the equivalent of Latin *ad vallum*, to the valley. But Skeat much more boldly quotes Florio who defines the Italian *valenzana* as "a kind of saye, serge or stuffe to make curteins for beds with," and says it was "probably named from Valence in France, not far to the south of Lyons, where silk is made even to this day." Johnson actually spells the word *valence*, and derives it "from Valencia in Spain, also famous for silk."

How then did Saint Valentine come to be associated with lovers, facetious or otherwise? One tradition, given by Butler, is that he or several other "zealous pastors" endeavoured "to abolish the heathen's lewd superstitious custom of boys drawing the names of girls, in honour of their goddess Februata Juno, on the 15th of this month," by substituting "the names of saints in billets given on this day." This, however, is reasoning backwards. That such a custom or "pious device" did at one time exist is supported by Blount who noted in 1656 that Valentines were "saints chosen for special patrons for a year, according to the use of the Romanists." But it was almost certainly introduced at "a relatively very late date," being mentioned for instance in the life of Saint Francis de Sales who died in 1622, and sounding like a desperate attempt to rescue a festival which had remained all too pagan for the Church.

Others have seen a connexion with the ancient Roman ceremony of Lupercalia, also performed on February 15. Its origin was attributed to Romulus and Remus, and it was said to honour the wolf (*lupus*) who suckled the famous twins. There is, however, no foundation for this story or for the existence of the god *Lupercus*, supposed to protect the flocks from wolves, who seems merely to have been invented to explain the feast. We remember it because it was "upon the Lupercal" that

G

Caesar was "thrice presented (with) a kingly crown." As for its
rites, they were very strange. Goats and a dog were sacrificed by
priests called Luperci, who were smeared with the bloody knife
and the blood wiped away with raw wool dipped in milk. It
was also essential that two of them must laugh. The Luperci
then cut thongs from the skins of their victims and ran in two
bands round the walls of the old Palatine city using them as
whips. A blow from the thongs was thought to be a sure cure for
sterility.

Pope Gelasius is said to have abolished the Lupercalia in
494 and replaced it by the feast of the Purification of the
Blessed Virgin Mary, commonly known as Candlemas, on
February 2. February indeed gets its name from the Latin
februo, to purify by sacrifice. But all this still brings us no nearer
to the problem of the valentine.

Perhaps Tennyson had the true explanation when he remarked that "in the spring a young man's fancy lightly turns
to thoughts of love." February 14 may be a little early for
spring, though sometimes there is a hint of it in the air. And
what does emerge in the fourteenth century is a persistent belief
that this was the day on which birds began to pair. Chaucer's
Parlement of Foules was held

> . . . on seynt Volantynys day,
> Whan every foul cometh ther to chese his make,
> Of every kinde, that men thenke may;
> And that so huge a noyse gan they make,
> That erth and see, and tree, and every lake
> So ful was, that unnethe[1] was ther space
> For me to stonde, so ful was al the place.

Shakespeare was making mild fun of this belief when Duke
Theseus remarks of the lovers in *A Midsummer Night's Dream*,

[1] scarcely.

Saint Valentine is past:
Begin these wood-birds but to couple now?

It has also been suggested, on what authority I do not know, that the *Puys d'Amour*, "a sort of eisteddfod for love-minstrels and troubadours," what Littré describes as *une assemblée de dames et de poétes*, were held "on this date in the twelfth century." These *puys*, says Larousse, although created to honour religious works, became more and more profane. And Charlotte M. Yonge, in her *History of Christian Names*, vastly entertaining if not always reliable, records the name Violante as "occurring in the South of France and the north of Italy and Spain . . . It may very probably be a corruption of some old Latin name such as Valentinus or . . . it may be from the golden violet, the prize of the troubadours in the courts of love."

Certainly France, at any rate, *dans plusieurs villes de province*, also had this practice of choosing a *valentin* or *valentine*, though it seems to have attached itself not to Saint Valentine's Day but to the *dimanche des brandons*. This was the first Sunday in Lent, so called from the *brandons* or bunches of flaming straw which were carried in procession on that day.

What then is or was a valentine? Quite definitely, when the custom first arose, a valentine was a person; someone "of the opposite sex chosen by lot or otherwise determined on Saint Valentine's Day, as a sweetheart, lover or special friend for the ensuing year." That there may have been some degree of seriousness in this choosing of valentines, sometimes even 'with a view to marriage', is shown by some charming letters which survive among the papers of the Paston family of Norfolk.

In February 1477 Elizabeth Brews wrote to her young relative John Paston on behalf of her daughter Margery, concerning a match which had already been proposed between the two: "And, cosyn, uppon Fryday is sent Volentynes Day, and every brydde[1]

[1] bird.

chesyth hym a make; and yf it lyke yow to com on Thursday at nyght, and so purvey yowe that ye may abyde ther tyll Monday, I trust to God that ye schall so speke to myn husbonde, and I schall prey that we schall bryng the mater to a conclusion." Whether he responded to this invitation is not clear. It seems unlikely, since Margery herself sent him a letter, also in February, addressed "Unto my ryght welbelovyd Voluntyn, John Paston, Squyer, be this bill delyvered," and the letter begins, "Ryght reverent and wurschypfull and my ryght welebeloved Voluntyne, I recommande me unto yowe full hertely, desyring to here of your welefare, which I beseche Almyghty God long for to preserve unto hys plesure and yowr hertys desyre. And yf it please yow to here of my welefare, I am not in good heele of body ner of herte, nor schall be tyll I here from yowe." And she signs herself, "Be your Voluntyne, Mergery Brews." It is nice to know that she got him in the end.

Incidentally these ladies' spelling of *voluntyne*, corresponding to Chaucer's *volantyne*, echoed the common pronunciation of the word. Even as late as 1878 an aged Lincolnshire lady remembered that in her childhood she always spoke of *vollantines*; "valentines we set down as an alien affectation."

Properly speaking this choosing of valentines took place on the previous evening. "It is," noted Bourne in 1725, "a ceremony never omitted among the Vulgar, to draw lots which they term Valentines, on the Eve before Valentine-Day." And here, from Morayshire in Scotland, is a first-hand account of the procedure observed which, though recorded in the nineteenth century, had probably changed little for hundreds of years: "A number of young people of the town or village assembled in some particular house for the purpose of drawing their valentines . . . A sheet of paper was cut up into slips sufficient in number for the boys or young men who were to put their fortune to the test. Upon these slips the names of the girls were written. When ready the slips were placed in a hat and well shaken together. Then the drawing took place. Slips for the girls were prepared in the same way." And the next morning everyone, "to establish his claim to his Valentine," had "to proceed to the Valentine's home to announce the event . . . This was the real original way of observing Valentine's Day and was undoubtedly a survival from pagan times."

Such a visit, made while it was still night, proved the undoing of the young girl in Ophelia's song, who "proceeded to the Valentine's home" and "announced the event" thus:

> To-morrow is Saint Valentine's day,
> All in the morning betime,
> And I a maid at your window,
> To be your Valentine;
> Then up he rose, and donn'd his clothes,
> And dupp'd the chamber-door;
> Let in a maid, that out a maid
> Never departed more . . .
> Quoth she, before you tumbled me,
> You promised me to wed:
> So would I ha' done, by yonder sun,
> An thou hadst not come to my bed.

Possibly, however, the young lady was observing a variant of the custom reported by Misson in 1718: "There is another kind of valentine; which is the first young Man or Woman that Chance throws in your way in the Street, or elsewhere on that Day," and this encounter, provided the parties were single, was supposed to lead to their marriage. Pepys describes how his wife, "at which I made good sport to myself, held her hands all the morning that she might not see the paynters that were at work in gilding my chimney-piece and pictures in my dining-room." No doubt, as Wright remarks, "a maiden of those times would be astute enough to avoid meeting anyone she did not wish to marry," a comment which underlines the irony of Shakespeare's poem.

By Pepys' time, however, the custom had lost any seriousness it might once have had and become an amusing and pleasant excuse for showing affection and exchanging gifts. On February 14, 1668, the diarist wrote, "Up, being called by Mercer (the Pepys' servant), who come to be my Valentine, and so I rose . . . and did give her a guinny in gold for her Valentine's gift. There comes also my cozen Roger Pepys betimes . . . to my wife, for her to be his Valentine." And the previous year he had noted, "This morning come up to my wife's bedside, I being up dressing myself, little Will Mercer, to be her Valentine." Will, the brother of Mercer, was at this time sixteen years old. He "brought her name writ upon blue paper in gold letters, done by himself, very pretty; and we were both well pleased with it."

Such gifts, also known as valentines, were not always so modest. On one occasion Mistress Pepys received from an admirer "half a dozen pairs of gloves and a pair of silk stockings and garters." And Samuel himself, who was his wife's permanent Valentine, "by arrangement to be so to her every year," wryly comments, "this year I find it is likely to cost £4 or £5 in a ring for her, which she desires." It was in fact "a Turquie ring set with diamonds," which he bought for her about a week later.

The word valentine also became attached to the folded pieces of paper "inscribed with the name of a person to be drawn as a valentine," and to draw valentines was "to draw lots for this or other reasons." This apparent frivolity even got itself included in a Scottish Act of Parliament of 1639, described as an "Act ordaining the Commissioners of shyris to draw lottis and valentines yeirlie at ilk parliament for thair places." Then there was the scandalous affair of King Charles I and the Lord Chancellor recorded in *Popular Antiquities*. When the King was at Edinburgh in 1641, "it was proposed to him that the Lord Chancellor should be chosen as they do valentines, and the King consented." As Sir Patrick Wemyss wrote to a friend, "It was moved amongst them that every man should give his voice, after the question was stated, in a piece of paper, and put them, like Valentines, in the clerk's hat; and so to be numbered. This his Majesty yielded to in the forenoon; but in the afternoon came to the House and told them that he had forgot himself, and entreated them to let that alone . . . But their hearts were hardened." Though this system seems to be no more than a kind of secret ballot, it was in any case eventually abandoned.

Regarding "the clerk's hat", it may perhaps be noted that the sporting term *handicap* is thought to have originated from the phrase *hand in cap*, or *hand i' the cap*. We first find it as the name of a pastime "with an element of chance in it, in which one person challenged some article belonging to another, for which he offered something of his own in exchange." An umpire was then chosen "to decree the difference of value between the two articles, and all three parties deposited forfeit money in a cap or hat." The umpire then announced his decision as to the compensation or 'odds' to be given with the inferior article, and the two parties indicated their acceptance or non-acceptance of the terms by drawing out their hands either with money in them or empty. "If the two were found to agree in holding the match 'on' or 'off', the whole of the money deposited (in the cap) was taken by the umpire; but if not, by the party who was willing that the match should stand." Handicap in this sense is a seventeenth-century word, but Langland much earlier gives a long account of a similar game played in a tavern and known as New Fair.

Soon races between two horses were being run on the same principle, "the umpire here decreeing the extra weight to be carried by the superior horse, and the parties drawing as above to declare whether the match should be on or off." Hence the cry that is raised in *John Gilpin*, "He carries weight, he rides a race!" In time the origin of the term was forgotten and handicap was thought to apply to the extra weight itself or any similar penalty imposed on a more favoured competitor. From this it came to mean "an encumbrance or disability that weighs upon effort and makes success more difficult," and nowadays *handicapped* is much used to describe anyone who faces life with the odds against him.

In sixteenth-century Scotland a valentine, perhaps from the way it was folded, could even be "a sealed letter from the Crown to landholders for the apprehension of persons offending against the law." A decree was issued about 1556 "for inbringin of certaine personis gevin in valentynis," which "valentynis" contained "the names of the personis culpable."

In spite of Will Mercer's "name writ upon blue paper in gold letters," and Pepys' own note in 1667, "Here do I first observe the fashion of drawing mottoes as well as names . . . What mine was I forget, but my wife's was, 'Most courteous and most fair,' which might be very pretty," it was not until the end of the eighteenth century that a card or letter came to take the place of the gift. Although the sender still continued to ask, "Dearest mine, will you be my Valentine?" or words to that effect, the name soon became transferred to the actual "written or printed letter or missive, a card of dainty design with verses or other words, especially of an amorous or sentimental nature, sent on Saint Valentine's Day to a person of the opposite sex."

Some of these cards were most elaborately made, with satin, silk and lace or hand-cut paper. A very early one is described as being "a pretty cut, hand-coloured, of a swain peeping through a hedge at his mistress, who, seated on a rustic bench, is reading his valentine, 'I want my dear maid a sweet partner for life; so tell me in earnest if you'll be my wife.'" Sometimes the sender signed his name, but it later became the fashion for valentines to be "perfectly anonymous," leaving the recipient to guess who was making love to her through the post. Perhaps young men thought it was safer that way; at least it protected them from actions for breach of promise.

The Victorian era, from about 1850 to 1880, was the heyday of the valentine. In February 1872 a newspaper reported, "We hear that about 150,000 letters passed through the Norwich Post Office from Tuesday evening to Wednesday evening." Nor were they all amorous or sentimental; quite in modern style, they could also be "comic, satirical, and vulgar or offensive," which last were "rarely enclosed in an envelope." The vogue, however, declined with the century, and the *Daily News* noted in 1898 that "the Christmas card has apparently killed the valentine . . . Valentines are still sold, and sent, but they are chiefly of the satirical order." The connexion seems a little strained, but it is interesting to observe that this was the general opinion: "the old valentine has been quite superseded by Christmas and picture post cards."

There was, however, something of a revival about 1930, though it may have been commercially prompted. "Messrs. Raphael Tuck and Sons Ltd . . . published a series of valentine cards" which sold quite well, and "the celebrations in the hotels," Valentine Balls and other similar functions, "were highly popular . . . At the Savoy there were more than 1,000 guests." And in 1936, Leap Year, when tradition allows the women to propose to the men, "the number of valentines sold was very great, and the Postmaster General issued special valentine telegram forms."

Apparently there is still enough trade in valentines today for manufacturers to continue to produce them; the *Daily Telegraph* reported in 1967 that "sales of Valentine cards are expected to be up . . . on last year, with no fewer than 20 million people buying cards to the all-in tune of £3 million." And in spite of what *The Times* called "the present proliferation of vulgar cards," the sentimental ones are still there and they still say, "Be my Valentine." But very few of the senders ever pause to remember Guy Crouchback's "steadfast clergyman . . . seventeen centuries back."

Indeed we have never had much devotion to him. Butler noted long ago that "although on account of the custom connected with his feast the name of Saint Valentine is very familiar in England, no church is known to have been dedicated in his honour in this country." Nor is it likely that since then the omission has been repaired.

Another and not obviously related tradition was that of *valentining*, when the children used to go from door to door, as they do in America at Hallowe'en, "and sing or repeat a few lines in order to obtain money, cakes or fruit." The cakes at one time were specially made, "sweet plum buns . . . called Valentine buns." And the verse, though it exists in many variants, was always essentially the same:

> Good morrow to you, Valentine.
> Curl your locks as I do mine,
> Two before and three behind.
> Good morrow to you, Valentine.

10

THOU ART PETER

Tu es petrus, et super hanc petram aedificabo ecclesiam meam. Laying aside its theological implications, this is a fascinating text, since it records the actual creation of one of the most popular Christian names throughout Europe and, as western culture spread, throughout much of the rest of the world. A moment before, Christ has addressed his disciple by his proper name Simon Bar-jona, Simon the son of Jona. He tells him he is a rock, or more correctly a stone—in Aramaic *Cephas*, in Greek *Petros*, in Latin *Petrus*—and the nickname stuck. Even the evangelists are never quite sure how to describe him; sometimes he is simply Simon, sometimes he is Simon called Peter, sometimes Simon Peter, Simon the Stone. Eventually the Simon disappears; to Saint Luke in *Acts* he is Peter only, and under that name he was canonized by the Church.

Petros in Greek is a stone, *petra* a rock; in Latin the equivalent words are *petrus* and *petra*. The pun upon Peter holds good in every language descended from Latin or Greek—Pierre, for instance, in France and Pietro in Italy. English, however, that linguistic rag-bag, has lost it. Our stone is a Germanic word, Old English *stān* or *stane*, our rock a version of French *roche*, from a later Latin *rocca*. In America, it is true, Rock has had a certain currency as a given name, though even here the connexion with Peter is not evident. We do preserve the Latin in many 'learned' words, from saltpetre—*sal petrae*, salt of the rock—to petrol, shortened from petroleum—*petrae oleum*, oil of the rock—to petrify, from French *pétrifier*, representing a supposed Latin *petrificare*, to turn to stone; but not in the straightforward rock or stone, which is a pity.

95

Saint Peter, perhaps because of his obvious humanity and his impetuous tendency always to say and do the wrong thing, appealed to the imagination of the mediaeval Church more than any other of the Apostles; in England alone there are said to be well over a thousand churches dedicated to him, from Westminster Abbey downwards, more than twice as many as to Saint Michael the Archangel, the next commonest. And the name appears in some form or other in almost every European language: Peter, Pers, Pierre, Per, Peer, Peder, Pieter, Piet, Pietro, Piero, Pedro, Petr, Pyotr, Picti, Petur, Pietar, Feoris.

The English form of Peter is a late development. As a baptismal name it seems to have come over with the Normans in the northern French spelling Piers. In the fourteenth century the eponymous hero of Langland's poem is Piers the Plowman, sometimes referred to as Perkin, though when he swears rather mildly it is "bi saynt Peter of Rome". For this reason nearly all our 'Peter' surnames are based on Piers and so are not always immediately recognisable: Pierson, son of Piers, with all its many variants Pearson, Piers, Pierce, Pearce, Pearse, Pears, Peers, Perse, Peres, Perris, Ferris; Parkinson from Perkin or Peterkin, Purkins, Perkins, Parkins; the Perrott, Parrot, Parrett, Porrett, Porritt group; Petre and from the West Country Pether, Pethers, Pither, Pithers. Petrie is Scottish and the more obvious Peterson or Peters are said to be almost always Welsh, since in Wales surnames were seldom adopted until the sixteenth century when the older Piers was giving way to Peter. Before that they used the patriarchal 'son of'—Owen ap Tudor, Owen son of Tudor, or Thomas ap Rhys. Ap Rhys, of course, developed into Price, an essentially Welsh patronymic.

A less usual English surname is Dampier. This also is French in origin and probably came over with the Normans, being "the name of numerous places in France, two of which are in Normandy". It is, according to Weekley, properly spelt

Dampierre, which stands for *Dominus Petrus*—Lord or Saint Peter.

The saint, says Brewer, "is usually represented as an old man, bald, but with a flowing beard, dressed in a white mantle and blue tunic, and holding in his hand a book or scroll. His peculiar symbols are the keys and a sword." To the Middle Ages he was known as "the Prince of the Apostles" and like any earthly prince he had his legitimate successors, the Bishops of Rome, the Popes.

That this association was recognised early in England is shown by the institution known as the *"Denarius Petri, anglice* Petir pens *vel* Romscot." This Peter or Peter's Pence was "an annual tax or tribute of a penny from each householder having land of a certain value, paid before the Reformation to the papal see of Rome." Robert of Gloucester reports in 1297 that "fram rome he broght an heste that we here nome[1] Petres peni of ech hous that smoke out of come." But the origin of the tax goes back at least five centuries earlier, some say to the time of Ine, King of Wessex, 688 to 728, or of Offa, King of Mercia, 755 to 794. It is certainly mentioned as due by ancient law in a Latin letter of King Canute, and seems to have been peculiar to England and other northern lands.

Although it was also known as Romescot, *scot* being the old name for a tax-payment, a contribution or even a fine, hence scot-free, there is no suggestion that this was a tribute actually levied by Rome. It appears to have been more of a free-will offering on the part of the Saxon kings, and continued to be paid until Henry VIII abolished it by statute in 1534, though not without increasing protest. As, for instance, when in 1376 the commons presented a petition to the king, Edward III, "stating that the taxes paid yearly by them to the pope amounted to five times the royal revenue." And Langland wanted a decree

[1] collect.

issued that "alle Rome-runneres" should "Bere no silver over see that signe of kynge sheweth, Noyther grave no ungrave, golde noither silver."

At first Peter's Pence was collected from every family, but later only those of some substance were expected to pay. Carte the historian stated in 1747 that the rate was "a penny by every family that had thirty pence annual rent in land"; other versions are "everyone who shall have thirty pence of current money in his house of his own property" or those "who had the value of thirty pence in quick or live stock". It was payable every year on August 1, the feast of Saint Peter ad Vincula or Saint Peter in Chains, also known as Petermas, and it "was thence called Peter-pence". It seems more probable, however, that the name meant simply the pence sent to the representative of Saint Peter in Rome. Catholic churches still have boxes labelled 'Peter's Pence', but this is now an entirely voluntary contribution to the Papal Treasury and no one is forced to pay, whether or not smoke comes out of his chimney and however much "current money" he may have in his house.

Because of its strong papist associations the name Peter fell out of favour at the time of the Reformation; to give it to your child would be almost a declaration of Catholic sympathies. It sank low in the social scale; already for Shakespeare it was a name for a servant, indeed the servant of a servant, since he attends on the Nurse in *Romeo and Juliet:* "My fan, Peter . . . Peter, stay at the gate." In the seventeenth and eighteenth centuries the name became very uncommon, and was thought of, as also in France, as "rustic and old-fashioned". The one 'aristocratic' literary character of the period who comes to mind is Sir Peter Teazle and even he is something of a fool.

The return of the name to general popularity, its Popish connexions forgotten or ignored, was, says the *Oxford Dictionary of English Christian Names*, "no doubt due largely to Barrie's

Peter Pan". This play, the most triumphant piece of whimsy ever
to hold the stage, was first produced in 1904. It appealed to all
that was infantile in the English character and after sixty years
appears to be doing so still.

Peter was named from one of Barrie's nephews, for whom he
created the story; Pan associates him with the goat-footed god,
but he has none of his characteristics except a habit of playing
on the pipes, a quality rather incorrectly known as 'feyness' and
a total dissociation from ordinary everyday life, emphasised by
his title of 'The Boy who would not grow up'. He is dressed,
"in so far as he is dressed at all . . . in autumn leaves and cob-
webs." He claims proudly, "I heard father and mother talking
of what I was to be when I became a man. I want always to be a
little boy and have fun; so I ran away . . . and lived among the
fairies." It may be some consolation to those whose name is
Peter to know that Webster defines a Peter Pan as "a person who
retains in mature years the naturalness of spirit and charm
associated with childhood"; but he also quotes the more sinister
view that he is one "who absolutely will refuse to escape from
the comfortable irresponsible stage of childhood." Psychiatrists
would almost certainly agree.

The considerable popularity of Wendy as a name for a girl is
also due to Barrie, since though he did not invent it he certainly
introduced it to the English public. In fact he saddled Peter's
girl-friend with a nickname of his own, evolved for him "by
W. E. Henley's little daughter Margaret". She used to call him
'Friendy', which soon became 'Friendy-wendy' and finally
'Wendy' *tout court*.

Peter has no obvious feminine form, unless it might be Petra,
which has had something of a vogue in recent years, though it is
chiefly famous as the name of an ancient Arabian city, so called
"from the long sandstone parapets which gird the Wady Mousa".
The early discovery of an ancient Roman tomb with the

inscription *Filiae dulcissimae Aureliae Petronillae* led, however, to
the persistent belief that this was Saint Peter's daughter, called
after her father Petronilla. More probably it is a diminutive of
Petronius, the name of a Roman *gens* or family, whose most
distinguished representative was Gaius Petronius, the *arbiter
elegantiae* of Nero's imperial court.

Nonetheless Petronilla has her story. She was another of the
countless virgins who looked on marriage as a fate worse than
death. According to the Roman Martyrology she "refused to
wed Flaccus, a nobleman, and accepting three days' delay for
deliberation, spent them in fasting and prayer, and on the third
day, after receiving the Sacrament of Christ, gave up the ghost."
A Roman fresco seems to support the idea that there may have
been a martyr of this name, but that she was the "daughter of the
blessed Apostle Peter" is merely fanciful. In spite of this quite a
cult in her honour grew up in the Middle Ages, and she was
particularly invoked, like her supposed father, against fevers,
no doubt because "when Jesus was come into Peter's house, he
saw his wife's mother . . . sick of a fever. And he touched
her hand and the fever left her." She was also the special
patroness of the Dauphins of France, "by reason of the dolphin
which was reputed found carved on her sarcophagus."

In England Petronilla was often shortened to Peronel, Pernel
or Parnel, names proverbial for "a gaily dressed bold-faced
woman" or even worse. The sin of Superbia or Pride is represented by Langland as "peronelle proude-hert", who wears a
luxurious "purfil", that is a dress with an embroidered or furred
trimming, from French *pourfiler*, "to work on an edge, to em-
broider with thread," and incidentally almost identical with
profile in origin. Pernel or Parnel was commonly used to describe
a priest's concubine, his *con cubina*, the person with whom he
lies down. Again Langland speaks of "Dame Peronell" being
"a prestes file", that is his girl, his *filia*, his *fille*; unfortunately

filly has another derivation, being Teutonic and related to *foal*.

From this Pernel was extended to mean any loose woman, a sense which it kept in dialect until the eighteenth century. It could also be applied to a woman who was over-sensitive; "Tender Parnell," says Grose, "a tender creature, fearful of the least puff of wind or drop of rain. As tender as Parnell, who broke her finger in a posset drink." Now it has disappeared, except as the surname Parnell.

Peter or Pierre in France as well as in England became a generic name for a rustic, a peasant, a comic clown or buffoon, especially in the slightly patronising form *Pierrot* or little Peter. And with Pierrot, "a character originally in French pantomime, representing a man in growth and a child in mind and manners, (who) is generally the tallest and thinnest man that can be got, has his face and hair covered with white powder or flour, and wears a white gown with very long sleeves and a row of big buttons down the front," we are once again in the world of the *Commedia dell' Arte*.

Although he cannot be traced back to Italy itself, Pierrot appears to have been created by an Italian actor, Giuseppe Giaratone, working with the Italian Company in Paris about 1665, and is probably related both to Pulchinella, a man with a woman's name, a hook nose and a hump, known to us as Mister Punch, and to the clown Pagliaccio of 'On with the Motley' fame, whose name is said to mean literally 'chopped straw'. These are all servant characters, of which there were two types. The first is "clever, apt, witty, one who can perplex, cheat, trick and delude everyone", the typical Harlequin, in fact. The second "must be foolish, clumsy, dull, so that he cannot tell his right hand from his left", and his costume is "a full white shirt, long loose white pantaloons, a peaked cap and a wooden sword." Giaratone took over this character, emphasised his rustic

H

simplicity and awkwardness, whitened his face, gave him a soft hat with a large floppy brim, sleeves which later grew to a ludicrous length, and a personality that lived for centuries.

After him came Gaspard Deburau, the brilliant mime, who for twenty years, says the *Oxford Companion to the Theatre*, "acted nothing else. Without speaking a word he mimed the naiveté, the clumsiness, the childish joys of this comic yet pathetic figure, who became almost legendary." This is the Pierrot of Fokine's ballet *Le Carnaval*, always hopeful, always disappointed desperately trying to catch butterflies in his hat. By the nineteenth century the character had changed again and not for the better. A certain Paul Legrand had made him "less amusing and more sentimental, a trait which was later developed by a host of imitators, until the robust country lad became a lackadaisical, love-sick youth pining away from unrequited love, and much addicted to singing mournful ballads under a full moon."

Although he had appeared in English pantomime and harlequinades for some time, his latest and oddest transformation was into what became known as the 'Pierrot troupe', a collection of singers, dancers and comedians, men and women, who generally 'entertained'. Their costume was usually a basic white and black, "the girls in short frilly white frocks, the men in loose black or white suits, with coloured buttons, ruffs and ruffles," and pom-poms too, I remember. They first burst upon England at Henley Regatta in the 1890s, and by 1904 the *Daily News* was reporting that "niggers at the seaside have . . . given place to pierrots." For years these concert parties were so ubiquitous in pier pavilions many people must have thought that was how they got their name; in fact a *pier*, says Skeat, is "a mass of stone work," and a pier glass once meant a mirror that "hung on the stonework between two windows" in a castle or a house. After the second war, when tastes grew more sophisticated, pierrots disappeared. But since minstrels have already made a comeback we may yet see them again.

Pierrot was and is also the French familiar name for a sparrow; in English at one time this bird was known as Philip, as can be seen from John Skelton's long elegy written

> For the soul of Philip Sparrow
> That was late slain at Carrow . . .
> Whom Gib our cat hath slain.

Birds especially were often christened in this way—Tom tit Jack daw, Robin redbreast, Jenny wren, Mag pie, Poll parrot— and the choice of name seems to have been purely arbitrary. Philip, Phip or Pip sparrow is one that has disappeared; Pip nowadays would be more likely to belong to a dog. But Byron, when he was feeling kindly towards her, called his wife Pip; I cannot help wondering if perhaps she was rather like a sparrow.

As for Polly or Poll parrot, this makes the creature into an hermaphrodite if, as seems possible, the elusive word *parrot* is really an anglicised version of French Perrot, yet another form of 'little Peter'. Parrot, meaning the bird, appears suddenly in English about 1525, and there is no other comparable word in any related language. Before this it was known as a *popinjay*, or any of the almost endless variety of spellings in which this word is found. It seems to go back through a Latin *papagallus* and a mediaeval Greek *papagos* to an Arabic *babbagha*, possibly re-presenting "an imitation of the cry of the bird in an African or other barbarian tongue". The rather unexpected *jay* at the end probably comes from confusion with that other harsh-voiced chattering bird, the European jay.

Eventually popinjay developed the secondary sense of a vain or conceited person. Thus Hotspur in *Henry IV* at the Battle of Holmedon complains of being "pester'd with a popinjay"—

. . . he made me mad
To see him shine so brisk and smell so sweet
And talk so like a waiting gentlewoman
Of guns and drums and wounds.

The allusion is probably to the splendour of the parrot's feathers and the pleasure it appears to take in the sound of its own voice.

The surnames Popegay, Popejoy or Pobjoy derive from this word, which sometimes is written *popegai* or *popingay*. They may represent "either a nickname from the bird or a title for the winner in the sport" which was described by Cotgrave at some length in the seventeenth century. This consisted of setting up a wooden parrot or *popegay* "on the top of a steeple, high tree or pole, whereat there is, in many parts of France, a general shooting once every year; and an exemption for all that year, from *la taille*, obtained by him that strikes down the right wing thereof (who is therefore tearmed *Le Chevalier*); and by him that strikes down the left wing (who is tearmed *Le Baron*); and by him that strikes down the whole popinjay (who for that dexteritie or good hap hath also the title of *Roy du Popegay*) all the year following." Nor is this exemption from tax as strange as it seems, for the idea was to train men who could if necessary act as soldiers, just as archery practice was at one time compulsory in England.

The difficulty of deriving *parrot* from Perrot, or indeed any other source, is that it seems to have sprung to life full-formed, without any history. There is no evidence of the use of Perrot in the French of the period as a nickname for the bird, and there is equally no evidence of Perrot occurring as a personal name in England. Somewhere the essential connexion has disappeared. All we do know is that Perot appears as an English surname in 1235, Parrat in 1344 and Parotte in 1470; these are clearly Peter-derivatives, but have no evident relation to the bird.

Yet its first known use, in Skelton's *Speke, Parrot*, begins triumphantly, "Parrot is my name, a bird of Paradise", and it seems clear from the poem that Parrot *is* his name, just as the sparrow was Philip. Whether Skelton chose it for himself or whether it was a use already fashionable we cannot know. Certainly he does not find it necessary to make any sort of explanation beyond describing his hero:

> With my beke bent, my little wanton eye,
> My feathers fresh as is the emerald green,
> About my neck a circulet like the rich ruby,
> My little legges, my feet both feat and clean,
> I am a minion to wait upon a queen.

What is even more remarkable, Skelton seems to have spelt it exactly as we do; there cannot be many words unchanged since their introduction yet over four hundred years old.

An equally puzzling word is *parakeet*. It came into English from French *perroquet*, the usual word for a parrot, or Spanish *periquito*. These birds were known to the ancient Greeks, who called them *psittakos*, hence our *psittacosis*, and also to the Romans, so the original form of the word may have been Italian; on the other hand it may have come from the Spanish and Portuguese navigators, who rediscovered the parakeet during their voyages. If it is Spanish it may be "a diminutive of the much commoner name *perico*, supposed to be the same word as *Perico*, a colloquial form of *Pedro*"—Peter again.

If it comes from Italy, however, its history may be much more bizarre. There are two common Italian forms, *parrochetto* or *parruchetto*. The first is said to derive from the *parroco* or parish priest, *parrochetto* being a little priest or parson, as the French call the sparrow a *moineau* or a little monk. The second form has been associated with *parruca* or *perruca*, a wig. This became in French *perruque* and was borrowed into English as *peruke*, but soon changed to *perewyke*, and finally to *periwig*. The first two syllables were dropped and we were left with *wig*, which is, in the linguistic sense, perfectly meaningless.

According to this theory the parakeet got its name because it was *un oiseau panaché* and the plumage on its head made it look as if it was wearing a *parruca* or wig. On the other hand Partridge suggests that "the Italian *perruca*, like Old Provençal *peruca*, perhaps meant originally 'with hair resembling a parrot's ruffled feathers'." Which came first, in fact, the parrot or the wig? Littré concludes that in the French spelling of *perroquet* there has been a confusion and mixture of *Perot*, *pierrot* and *perruque*, and this seems as far as we are likely to get.

Another bird that is almost certainly called after Saint Peter is the petrel, "a small sea-bird *Procellaria pelagica*, with black and white plumage and long wings", which birds, according to the French naturalist Buffon, "sometimes hover over the water like swallows, and sometimes appear to run on top of it." This again is a word which occurs first in English; to be precise, in 1676 when a sailor "saw many pitterals about the ship". By 1703, however, Dampier uses the spelling *petrel*, and comments on it thus: "As they fly . . . they pat the water alternately with their feet, as if they walkt upon it; tho still upon the wing. And from hence the seamen give them the name of Petrels, in allusion to Saint Peter's walking upon the Lake of Gennesareth."

If Dampier's derivation is accepted, this is another word meaning 'little Peter'. Perhaps the earliest form should have been not *pitteral* but *peterel*, in which case it might be similar to words like *cockerel*, a young cock, *pickerel*, a young pike, *doggerel*—no, not a young dog, but "ill-constructed or mean verse . . . presumably from *dog*, with contemptuous implication as in dog-Latin." (And though it is entirely irrelevant I cannot resist quoting Brewer's example of this language, the legal definition of a kitchen as "camera necessaria pro usus cookare: cum sauce-pannis, stewpannis, scullero, dressero, coalholo, stovis, smoak-jacko; pro roastandum, boilandum, fryandum et plum-pudding-mixandum.") Peterel would then be a diminutive of Peter; Skeat mentions a letter written by Buffon "dated 1782, who gives his opinion that (the French) *pétrel* is a better spelling than *peterel* because the derivation is from the name Peter, which is pronounced, he says, as *Pétre*." This would seem to confirm that the word came into French from English or German.

On the other hand it could have come from a Latin diminutive of Peter: *Petrillus* perhaps or *Petrellus*. Or it could have come from some entirely unconnected source represented by the original *pitteral*—it would be easy to imagine that the bird pittered or went pit-a-pat, took "quick light steps" with its feet—and that "the association with Peter was due to popular etymology". If so, however, it is not peculiar to England; that the petrel is known in Norway as *Pedersfugl* and in Germany as *Petersvogel* lends at least some support to the connexion with the impetuous man who said, "Lord, if it be thou, bid me come to thee on the water. And he said, Come. And when Peter was come down out of the ship, he walked on the water, to go to Jesus. But when he saw the wind boisterous, he was afraid; and be-ginning to sink, he cried, saying, Lord, save me."

Certainly sailors have always believed these birds to be harbingers of bad weather, as their name of Stormy Petrels emphasises. Captain Marryat in *Poor Jack* sets down the old belief, which also applies to gulls because of their eerie, plaintive cries, that they were the souls of sailors shipwrecked or drowned at sea, and "they are now the sailors' friends, come to warn us of the approaching storm". The phrase is sometimes used metaphorically of someone "whose activity is a sign of impending discord", who, as Brewer says, "can be calculated upon to 'raise Cain' wherever he goes, or whatever he does," or who seems to delight in strife and controversy. Thus the *Saturday Review* opined in 1862 that Monsieur Victor Hugo "is the petrel of literature, revelling in the storms of passion, and the conflict of the elements that determine human action."

Marryat also relates at some length the superstition that these birds should never be killed; and if they are, "it is certain that one of the crew must die and be thrown overboard to become a Mother Carey chicken to replace the one that has been destroyed." Mother Carey, according to sailors, had both chickens and geese, the latter being "the great black petrel or fulmar of the Pacific", and when it snows and the feathers flutter down she is said to be plucking her geese.

Who Mother Carey was, however, has never been established; the only other Carey I know of in English is Carey Street, in which one used to find oneself when one was bankrupt. Even Weekley admits defeat; he concedes that this is "probably a nautical corruption of some old Spanish or Italian name, but in spite of ingenious guesses this lady's genealogy remains . . . obscure." As for the ingenious guesses, the only one I have discovered is that of Brewer, upheld by Partridge, that this is a popular rendering "of the Latin *Mater Cara* (dear mother), a synonym for the Virgin Mary, regarded as the protector of sailors, by whom the 'chickens' . . . were formerly held in superstitious affection." Brewer supports his theory by adding that "the French call these birds *oiseaux de Notre Dame* or *aves Sanctae Mariae*", but I can find no confirmation of this; the only name Littré gives for the petrel is *oiseau des tempêtes*. Nor is there any comparable invocation in the Litany of the Blessed Virgin Mary; to sailors she is most commonly *Stella Maris*, Our Lady Star of the Sea.

Like most saints, Peter also has his plants. Peter grass was an old name for the wild thyme, and Peterwort, Herb Peter or Peter *per se* for the cowslip, because the flowers are like a bunch of keys; "Peter or cowsloppe, *herba Petri*", as a fifteenth-century manuscript records. Perhaps the most interesting, however, is Peter's Cress or *Crithmum maritimum*, more commonly known as samphire.

This plant, "the aromatic fleshy leaves of which are used in pickles", was catalogued by Elyot in 1545 as "*Crethmos vel Cretamus*, an herbe growing on the sea rocks, which we call sampere." From this and the other older spellings—sampiere, sampire, samper—it is much easier to spot the possible derivation, our modern form having almost certainly been influenced by *camphire*, the typical spelling of *camphor* down to the eighteenth century. Camphor has been altered by some zealous etymologist to conform with the mediaeval Latin *camphora*. Samphire, however, apparently escaped his attentions.

It came, of course, as Cotgrave noted in 1611, from the French *herbe de Saint Pierre*, literally Saint Peter's herb. This, oddly enough, was translated back into Latin, since the herbalists, like the botanists of today, used this language as the basis for an international nomenclature. So we find *sampetra* in 1616, and in 1694 *herba divi Petri*. The German name for this plant, *Meerpeterlein*, has something of the same idea. Samphire, as Partridge explains, "often grows upon cliffs and rocks. Saint Peter was by Christ himself associated with the rock of faith and by etymology with all rocks."

Shakespeare in *King Lear*, describing the cliffs at Dover, says:

> How fearful
> And dizzy 'tis to cast one's eyes so low!
> The crows and choughs that wing the midway air
> Show scarce so gross as beetles; half way down
> Hangs one that gathers samphire, dreadful trade!
> Methinks he seems no bigger than his head.

And though most modern editors print *samphire*, what he actually wrote was *sampire*, which is much more etymologically correct. This passage always used to trouble me, for I knew samphire, I had seen it growing, but always on what were called saltings or sea-marshes. I couldn't imagine what it was doing halfway down a chalk cliff.

Crabbe, however, solved my problem. Writing of *The Borough*, which is Aldeburgh in Suffolk, the town of Peter Grimes, and the broad, lazy estuary of the river Alde, he says:

> Here sampire-banks and salt-wort bound the flood;
> There stakes and sea-weeds, withering on the mud;
> And higher up, a ridge of all things base,
> Which some strong tide had rolled upon the place.

Anyone who has ever smelt the mud-flats can taste them in those lines. He too, as late as 1810, is using the old spelling. And he supplies his own note: "I.e., the jointed glasswort. *Salicornia* is here meant, not the true sampire, the *Crithmum maritimum*."

This the *OED* confirms, stating that samphire is also "a name for various other maritime plants, especially the glasswort, *Salicornea herbacea*." This "leafless plant with jointed stems, and an appearance suggestive of a small cactus or prickly pear, is common in salt-marshes in Britain. It makes a good pickle or antiscorbutic salad," and gets its name from the fact that it contains "a large amount of alkali, and on that account (was) formerly used in the manufacture of glass." The *OED* quotes, of all things, the *Western Gazette* as remarking in 1907 that "the glasswort is still called 'samphire' in Suffolk, and is gathered for purposes of pickling." Fifty years later this statement was still true; in the summer of 1965 I saw a notice on the coast of north Norfolk, 'Samphire for sale'. Only here they pronounce it to rhyme with camphor—samfer.

I I

PETERMEN AND PETARDS

Saint Peter as a patron must be very busy. He has under his care not only fishermen, as might be expected, but also bakers, bridge-builders, butchers, carpenters, clock-makers, fishmongers, glaziers, masons, netmakers, potters, stationers and ship-wrights. Though his connexion with some of these seems some-what tenuous, at least the fishermen and netmakers should be entitled to special consideration. For "as he walked by the sea of Galilee, he saw Simon and Andrew his brother casting a net into the sea; for they were fishers. And Jesus said unto them, Come ye after me, and I will make you to become fishers of men. And straightway they forsook their nets and followed him."

Nonetheless they seem from time to time to have gone back to them, no doubt as a means of livelihood when all else failed. Even after the resurrection Simon Peter with some half dozen of the disciples tells them, "I go a fishing," and they answer, "We also go with thee." But when Jesus appears to them on the shore Peter, impatient as ever, "girt his fisher's coat unto him (for he was naked) and did cast himself into the sea," while the others "came in a little ship . . . dragging the net with fishes." Andrew, James and John were all fishermen, so quite probably were others of the disciples. And yet it is always Peter whom we remember.

About 1400 it was decreed by the Common Council of London that none should "fish in the Thames with anglys nor other engines, but only with nets of assize and only at times seasonable, nor near any wharf of the bridge"—the bridge being London Bridge, the only one then built. The title of this decree is, "An Acte concernyng Peter-men and other fysshing in the Thames." Partridge quotes Bailey as having defined a peterman in the seventeenth century as "one who uses unlawful engines in catching fish on the river Thames". An engine, of course, is merely a clever contrivance, mechanical or otherwise, one showing *ingenium* or ingenuity. The *OED*, however, is not so categoric or else the sense has broadened; a Peterman, "apparently from Peter, in allusion to the occupation of Simon Peter," is now "a fisherman, formerly apparently one who practised a particular kind of fishing." It was also, incidentally, some kind of beer—"Give him a dram, or a glass of peterman"—but this is one of those ghost words that suddenly appear and equally suddenly vanish, without any ascertainable history.

But why should peterman and the comparable peterboat be local names, used chiefly on the Thames and the coasts about its estuary? There is at least one connexion between Saint Peter and the fishermen of the Thames, and it lies in the story of the founding of Westminster Abbey, as related by the monks of that Benedictine house as early as the eleventh century.

In the days, it is said, of Ethelbert, King of Kent, that is at the beginning of the seventh century, a rich citizen of London, perhaps Sibert, King of the East Saxons, built a church to Saint Peter on Thorney or Thorn Island, then a marshy waste some distance to the west of the City and known as *locus terribilis*, the terrible place. "The Saxons called it Thorney," says Stow, "because it was overgrowne with thorns and environed with water." Saint Mellitus, the Bishop of London, "came to consecrate the building, and pitched his tent in the neighbourhood" to be ready for the ceremony next morning.

That same evening, however, Saint Peter in person "appeared on the further bank of the river to a fisherman, who ferried him across." As he entered the church its windows glowed with heavenly light, though as a Saxon building and probably of wood it is not likely to have had very many. Then, aided by a celestial choir of angels to provide the singing and with, presumably, the fisherman as congregation, the apostle carried out the consecration, "being careful to leave the mystic Greek and Latin letters of the ritual traced in the dust to show that the rite had been well and canonically accomplished." The fisherman, having been rewarded in the true tradition of the miraculous draught of fishes "with an ample haul of salmon," was sent to inform Mellitus about what had occurred. He, instead of being righteously annoyed at such goings on behind his back, merely went to look and "when he had seen the signs of consecration, departed."

It seems, in its secrecy, an oddly pointless story, except that the monks were claiming their patron's particular favour. By this time, of course, they had another saint, Edward the Confessor, who certainly refounded the Abbey and built for it a great stone church in place of the older, smaller one. But there are in the pavement of the Chapter House designs of salmon to commemorate this story—and salmon were caught in the Thames up to quite recent times. Moreover, Saint Peter is said to have promised the London fishermen "never failing catches and told them to give one tenth of these towards the support of the community of the Abbey." In return for these contributions "they had the right of dining once a year with the Prior and monks", a right they are said to have exercised at least as late as 1387. There is no evidence that these diners were known as petermen, but they might have been.

Some of the fishermen certainly made use of peternets, "a kind of fishing net," though how these differed from other species of nets is not exactly clear. Day in 1880 described peternets as having "floats along the upper rope and weights along the footline, one end is attached on shore, and the other anchored out at sea on a right line with the coast," so they were used for off-shore rather than deep-sea fishing. Moreover, according to a regulation of 1584, they "must be two Inches large in the Meish." But what fish were caught with them and who employed them I haven't yet been able to establish.

Then there were peterboats, again "a local name, chiefly on the Thames and adjacent coasts," for a "decked fishing-boat smaller than a smack or a yawl". Brewer, writing in the 1860s, records that "they are still in common use round the mouth of the Thames, and were so called from Peterman, a term up to the eighteenth century for a fisherman." Their peculiarity was that they were double-ended, "made to go either way, the stem and stern being alike". Similar boats, according to Mayhew in his famous work on *London Labour and the London Poor*, were used by the dredgermen or river-finders, men who "bring up objects from the bed of a river, sea, etc., by dragging the bottom, using an iron frame with a net, bag or bucket attached," or in other circumstances who dredge up and sell oysters and other shellfish from the seabed. Their boats, says Mayhew, "are of a peculiar shape. They have no stern but are the same fore and aft. They are called Peter boats."

As well as legitimate dredgermen or dredgemen there were illegitimate ones, included in Mayhew's final volume, *They that Will not Work*. "These are men who are in the habit of going out early in the morning, as the tide may suit, for the purpose of dredging from the bed of the (Thames) coals which are occasionally spilled . . . when being transferred into the barges. If these parties are not successful . . . they invariably go alongside a loaded barge and carry off coals and throw a quantity of mud over them, to make it appear as if they had got them from the bed of the river." They were also known as fishermen; there is a strong connexion between petermen, fishermen and thieves, as will appear.

Another and much more widespread nautical association is the famous Blue Peter, "a blue flag with a white square in the centre," representing the letter P in the International Code of Signals. When flown singly, says the *Dictionary of Nautical Terms*, it denotes that "the vessel hoisting it is about to sail, and all persons concerned are to repair on board." At one time it was flown by the Navy for twenty-four hours before sailing "so that tradesmen could present their bills." According to the National Maritime Museum, "the first known mention of the name occurs in a poem written by Lady Hamilton, probably in April 1801, which would seem to imply that it was in common use at that time":

> Silent grief and sad forebodings
> (Lest I ne'er should see him more),
> Fill my heart when gallant Nelson
> Hoists Blue Peter at the fore.

According to Brewer, "it has been suggested that 'peter' here is a corruption of the French *partir* (leave or notice of departure)", or that "it takes its name from a 'repeater', a naval flag hoisted to indicate that a signal has not been read and should be repeated, this flag having been used with this meaning originally." But these, as he is the first to admit, "are both guesswork", as is the idea that "it is a corruption from some such expression as a blue pierced flag." Nobody really knows.

There is, however, no doubt about Saint Peter's fish. When Christ was asked for the tribute money he told Peter, "Go thou to the sea, and cast an hook, and take up the fish that first cometh up; and when thou hast opened his mouth, thou shalt find a piece of money: that take, and give unto them for thee and me." And the fish that Peter caught some say was a haddock, some say a John Dory, the *dorée* or golden fish. This latter, says Brewer, "is called in French *le poisson de Saint Pierre*, and in Gascon, the *golden* or *sacred cock*, meaning Saint Peter's cock. Like the haddock, it has an oval black spot on each side (near the pectoral fin), said to be the fingermarks (or finger and thumb) of Saint Peter when he held the fish to extract the coin." With crushing common sense, however, Brewer adds, "It is a pretty story, but haddocks cannot live in the fresh water of the Lake of Gennesaret."

Because they picked up money, Saint Peter's fingers were also "the fingers of a thief". Again according to Brewer, "they say a thief has a fishhook on every finger". But a *peterman* was in the canting lingo and is in modern slang a very specialised kind of thief.

It is at the end of the seventeenth century that we begin to hear of a *peter* being "in thieves' cant a portmanteau or trunk, a bundle or parcel of any kind," or, as Grose says more particularly, "a portmanteau or cloke-bag". The *portemanteau*, at one time a French official who carried a prince's mantle or loose sleeveless cloak, had come to mean a kind of bag in which coats or clothes were packed. Trying to find origins for cant words is about as profitable as looking for pots of gold at the foot of the rainbow, since they are, as Harrison remarks, "odde words of their own devising, without all order or reason", but in one of the several attempts Partridge makes at this one he suggests that peter "could be a disguise shortening of *portmantua*", one of many common spellings, "via the solecistic pronunciation *portmanter*".

From peter comes the *peter-lay*, "Rogues who follow Petty Thefts, such as cutting Portmanteaus etc. from behind Coaches", and the thief himself who was known as a *peterman* or *biter of peters*, "one that makes it a trade to steal boxes and trunks from behind stage coaches or out of waggons", while to "cut off the Cloak-bag or Port-manteau" was to "flick the Peeter". Although Mayhew, writing in the 1850s, does not seem to know the word peterman, and calls these thieves *dragsmen*, "those who steal goods or luggage from carts and coaches", he gives a good

description of how they went to work: "They run up and leap on the spring of the conveyance while the driver is proceeding along with his back toward them, lower the trunk, or other article from the roof, and walk off with it. These trunks some-times contain money, silver plate, and other valuable property . . . The wearing apparel in the trunks they sell at second-hand shops kept by Jews and others in low neighbourhoods such as Petticoat Lane, Lambeth, Westminster and the Borough of Southwark."

So much of this thieving went on that those travelling by coach had specially strong chains made to fasten their baggage down. The answer of the petermen was to design a small crow-bar for smashing the chains, called a *peter-hunting jemmy*, jemmy itself being "a familar form of James". This "small iron crow," explained Vaux in his *Flash Dictionary* of 1812, "was particularly adapted for breaking the patent chain with which the luggage is of late years secured to gentlemen's carriages; and which, being of steel, case-hardened, is fallaciously supposed to be proof against the attempts of thieves."

A later development of this game, recorded by Marrison in 1894, was *peterclaiming*, "laying hands nonchalantly on un-considered parcels and bags on railway stations". But this was a trick the passengers soon got wise to; they "sat defiantly on piles of luggage . . . and there was never a *peter* to touch for."

Nowadays petermen or petemen, as they are sometimes known in America, have turned their attention elsewhere. They are safe-breakers or safe-crackers, and a peter has become a strong box or a safe, a meaning which it acquired in the nine-teenth century. Partridge quotes an American definition of 1934: "A peter is a safe made from toolproof steel and usually has safety linings made from a special sort of cement." He adds that this is "the predominant twentieth century sense in Britain," and produces two further and slightly contradictory ideas about

I

how it acquired this name; either because a peter is something "as firm as a rock", or "perhaps because (it is) frequently 'netted' by thieves in allusion to Simon Peter's occupation". The first derivation, which is probably the generally accepted one, seems to ignore the earlier meaning of peter as a parcel or bag; the second would be much more appropriate to these than to a safe, which petermen normally break open rather than steal.

Again Mayhew does not seem to know this term, since to him safe-breakers, like "the higher burglars", are "termed the *cracksmen*". Grose, two centuries earlier, had recorded that "the Crack Lay, of late, is used in the cant language, to signify the art and mystery of house-breaking", though he has no cracksmen, only *crackmans*, which are hedges. With his usual thoroughness Mayhew describes the tool with which the cracksmen went to work: "A cutter for iron safes, an implement made similar to a centre-bit, in which drills are fixed. They fasten this into the key-hole by a screw with a strong pressure outside, the turning part so fixed that the drills cut a piece out over the key-hole sufficiently large to get to the wards of the lock. They then pull the bolt of the lock back and open the door." This implement, he says, is called a *petter-cutter*. But it seems quite reasonable to believe he got it wrong and it was really a peter-cutter.

While the cracksman or thief was at his work, his companion would keep watch, or *stand peter*. Partridge quotes a reference to this phrase as early as 1741; "Flack went in and took the goods, and I stood Peter on the Outside", which is glossed as "To stand Peter, in the language of these unhappy wretches, signifies to lie on the Watch." Again his suggested derivation is "from Peter of the rock-like faith?" But this is a game at which anyone can play. When Jesus was taken to the palace of the high priest, says Saint John, "Peter stood at the door without." And again, when Jesus went "unto a place called Gethsemani" he took with him Peter and James and John, and said to them, "Tarry ye here and watch." The only trouble is that such hindsight supposes an unexpectedly thorough knowledge of the Scriptures among latter-day thieves.

If, as often happens in twentieth-century America, there is a watchman to guard the safe, he can sometimes be disposed of by giving him "knock-out drops", also known as *peter*. "In five minutes he'll have the peter in his drink," quotes Partridge, and explains this as a pun—"Knock-out drops render a robbery *safe* for the robber, a safe is a *peter*." This connexion with safe may also account for the use of peter in America to mean a prison cell —a place as hard to break out of as a strong room is to break into.

One fact at least is clear among all this confusion; the modern peterman is a bank robber and a safe blower, especially one who employs explosives to get at his objective. Now at one time there was "a kind of firework with a loud report, a cracker", which was known as a *petard*. A petard was also "a small engine of war used to blow in a door or to make a breach in a wall". These explosions were caused by gunpowder, one of the chief constituents of which is saltpetre, also known as petre or peter. And yet all the evidence points entirely away from any connexion between *peter* and *petard*.

Johnson, quoting a contemporary *Military Dictionary*, gives a detailed description of the petar or petard as "an engine of metal, almost in the shape of an hat, about seven inches deep and about five inches over at the mouth: when charged with fine powder well beaten, it is covered with a madrier or plank, bound down fast with ropes, running through handles, which are round the rim near the mouth of it: this *petard* is applied to gates or barriers of such places as are designed to be surprised, to blow them up: they are also used in counter-mines to break through into the enemy's galleries."

The use of mine and counter-mine was quite a common

tactic in seventeenth-century siege warfare, one side digging
tunnels and the other side burrowing beneath and blowing them
up. This is what Hamlet has in mind when he says of those two
complaisant plotters Rosencrantz and Guildenstern,

> They must sweep my way,
> And marshal me to knavery. Let it work;
> For 'tis the sport to have the enginer
> Hoist with his own petar: and it shall go hard
> But I will delve one yard below their mines,
> And blow them at the moon—

a promise which, indeed, he faithfully keeps by changing the
warrant for his own death to a warrant for theirs, merely remarking to Horatio,

> 'Tis dangerous when the baser nature comes
> Between the pass and fell-incensed points
> Of mighty opposites.

The phrase 'hoist with his own petar' became at one time almost
proverbial, and this one reference of Shakespeare's still keeps the
word alive, even if something of a museum piece.

Florio notes the Italian word *petardo* in 1598, "a squib or
petard of gunpowder used to burst up gates or doores with."
These 'engines of war' were at first made of metal and bell-
shaped; some people even went in for do-it-yourself, as Ben
Jonson records: "He has made a petarde of an old brasse pot,
to force your dore." The spelling *petar* is Spanish, but our word
seems to have come from French *pétard*, since its origin is
French and rather unexpected—*péter*, to break wind. The
corresponding noun *pet* was at one time in use in English,
though rare and now obsolete. Littré, with his genius for definition, says it signifies *vent qui sort par en bas avec bruit*, for which
Webster substitutes more politely "an expulsion of intestinal

gas". Partridge comments that "this does not suggest a very great explosion"; what it does suggest is a soldiers' joke among the old sweats of the French artillery or sappers during the long tediums of some sixteenth-century war.

Camden in 1614 wrote of "Petronils, Pistoll, Dagge, etc., and Petarras of the same brood, lately invented". With *petronils* or *petronels* it would seem that we are back again with Petronilla, but this is far from the case. A petronel is "a large horse pistol . . . or horseman's piece", and is said to have been invented in the Pyrenees, presumably on the French side, for it is also recorded in the spelling *poictrinal* by Godefroy who says "it was fired by resting the butt-end against the chest." This makes it a form of French *poitrinal*, "of or belonging to the chest or breast", from Old French *peitrine*, later *poitrine*, the Latin *pectus*, breast.

In Italy, however, there were troopers known as *pietranelli*, "soldiers serving on horseback, well armed with a pair of cuirasses and weaponed with a fire-lock-piece or snaplance or a petronell". This allows Partridge, game to the last, to suggest that after all the derivation may be Italian, petronel being originally "*pietronello*, shortened to *petronello*, from *petra*, *pietra*, a stone, hence the flint for a gun".

If this were true it might perhaps equally relate to the opprobrious nickname Peter Gunner, said to be a slang term for "an amateur gun". Grose records that "Peter Gunner, will kill all the birds that died last summer", was "a piece of wit commonly thrown out at a person walking through a street or village near London, with a gun in his hand." The *OED* tentatively relates it to *peter* as a shortening of saltpetre, then gives a quotation which might seem, perhaps fortuitously, to connect it with petard. The year 1614 was known as the Cold Year, when frost and snow persisted and, just as in 1963–4, wild animals and birds were frozen and starving. "It was a shame," says an indignant chronicler, "that poore harmless Birds could not be suffered in such pitifull cold weather to save themselves under a Bush . . . but that every paltrie Peter gunner must fart Fire and Brimstone at them." But *fart* is an Anglo-Saxon word *feartan* or *feortan*, Middle English *verten*, as in the famous "Bulluc sterteth, bucke verteth, Murie sing cuccu!" and seems to be of Germanic origin, related to the Greek *perdein*, while *péter*, and hence petard, comes from Latin *pedere* and is said to be unconnected, though there are similar words in many ancient tongues.

As for the verb *to peter*, its earliest meaning in English is, rather strangely, to apply cosmetics, to paint the face, and the paint itself was *peter* also. Haliwell writes in 1689 of "Modish Women", each of whom has "her boxes of Peeter, and patches, and all her ornamental knacks and dresses". This use was ephemeral, as also the next meaning of to peter, being "to cease, stop or leave off". Vaux records "Peter that!" as being "synonymous with Stow that!" and the word is "slang, origin unknown". So is our modern use, though it has become of late years respectable and literary—to peter out, meaning "to diminish gradually and cease, to run out and disappear (as a stream or vein of ore), to die out, give out, fail, come to an end". It seems to have started life among American miners, probably in the silver-mines of the west or the gold-mines of the north, and no less a man than Abraham Lincoln gave it polite currency when he said, as his biographer records, that "the store in which he clerked was 'petering out', to use his own expression."

TEARS OF THE TANKARD

According to Saint Luke, Jesus once dined in the house of a Pharisee, and as he sat at table, "behold, a woman in the city, which was a sinner . . . brought an alabaster box of ointment, and stood at his feet behind him weeping, and began to wash his feet with tears, and did wipe them with the hairs of her head, and kissed his feet, and anointed them with the ointment." Simon the Pharisee was shocked that Christ should let himself be touched by a 'sinful' woman, the euphemism implying she was a prostitute or a harlot. But he, reading Simon's thoughts, answered him, "Her sins, which are many, are forgiven; for she loved much."

Saint John tells a similar story of Mary, the sister of Martha and Lazarus, who took "a pound of ointment of spikenard, very costly, and anointed the feet of Jesus, and wiped his feet with her hair: and the house was filled with the odour of the ointment." But he places the incident at Bethany only a week before Christ's death, instead of at the beginning of his ministry.

On a third occasion a woman or women came to anoint the body of Christ, this time after the crucifixion; "And they . . . prepared spices and ointments . . . and came unto the sepulchre bringing the spices which they had prepared." Among them or some say alone, was a certain Mary Magdalene, or as Saint Luke describes her, "Mary called Magdalene, out of whom went seven devils," and who now followed Christ "and ministered unto him of (her) substance."

One of the chief troubles about the Gospels, at least to

modern readers, is their lack of specificity, and also perhaps the number of women called Mary. "Even the earliest writers," says Charlotte M. Yonge, "were at a loss whether to identify the meek contemplative Mary of Bethany with the woman that was a sinner . . . and with Mary Magdalen, once possessed by seven devils and afterwards first witness of the Resurrection. While enquiry was cautious, legend was bold, and threw the three into one without the slightest doubt." And so, inextricably confused, they have remained, though not in the Eastern church, where Mary of Bethany is one person and Mary Magdalene, Mary the Myrrh-Bearer, quite another.

Since the word Magdalene itself "is believed to be a mere adjective of place, meaning she came from Magdala, which, in its turn, means a tower or castle," and was a village "on the western side of the Sea of Galilee, near Tiberias," it seems likely that she was called Mary of Magdala "to distinguish her from Mary of Bethany, with whom she is confounded." This, however, was no obstacle to the legend-makers, who supplied her with a whole biography.

Tradition, even less reliable than usual, says "that she was affianced to Saint John the Evangelist when Christ called him. She had therefore indignation that her husband was taken from her, and went and gave herself to all delight; but because it was not fitting that the calling of Saint John should be the occasion of her damnation, therefore our Lord mercifully converted her to penance." Before this, however, her "vain and sinful career" is described in detail, "her luxury, her robes, and in especial her embroidered gloves and flowing hair, and all the efforts of Martha to convert her." At last she is "healed of evil spirits" and "appears in Western hagiology as a harlot restored to purity and elevated to saintship by repentance and faith." According to Butler, "it was to the abused flesh of the penitent that the radiant and glorified body of the Son of God was first made manifest" after the resurrection. And it is interesting that on this occasion he says to her, *Noli me tangere*, touch me not.

In France it is believed that "she, with Lazarus, Martha and others" set out on a mission to Provence, landing at Les Saintes Maries de la Mer. Martha went on to Tarascon, where "by holding up the cross, (she) demolished a terrific dragon," the Tarasque, and where her tomb may still be seen, while Mary, "after having aided in converting the country, retired to a frightful desert, with a skull for her only companion." This desert was a cave at La Sainte Baume, high up in the Alpes Maritime, and here she died. Eastern tradition rejects this tale, saying instead that she was reunited with Saint John, went with him to Ephesus and died there. But in Ephesus itself the story goes that he was accompanied by Mary the Mother of Jesus, entrusted to his care by Christ on the cross.

"It is the legendary Magdalen," says Charlotte M. Yonge, "whom painters loved to portray in all her dishevelled grief, and whose title was applied first in France and then in England to homes for the reception of penitents like her supposed self." Magdalene in French became *Madeleine*, as in the famous *Eglise de la Madeleine* in Paris; *les filles de la Madeleine* or *Madelon-nettes* was a name given early *aux femmes de mauvaise vie retirées ou enfermées dans un couvent consacré à sainte Madeleine*. The same name was also given to the order of nuns in whose convents these 'fallen women' were received and cared for. In Paris the house of the Madelonnettes was in 1789 situated near the Temple. It was transformed into a prison during the Revolution and demolished as late as 1866.

In England Magdalene, meaning "a reformed prostitute, and . . . a house either of refuge or of reform for prostitutes," does not appear before the seventeenth century. Bailey in 1737 speaks of "Magdalens, an order of nuns, or rather worn out and penitent courtezans at Rome, upon whom a revenue was settled by Pope Clement VIII (1592–1605)." But it was not until 1758 that a plan was drawn up "for establishing a Charity-House . . . for the reception of repenting prostitutes, to be called the Magdalen Charity . . . in Goodmans Fields." By 1766 it was in operation: "In Prescot-street . . . we find a modern institution . . . founded by the name of Magdalen." And already by 1792 that uncompromising free-thinker Mary Wollstonecraft Godwin was proclaiming with force and considerable justice that such 'charity' was not enough: "Many innocent girls . . . are 'ruined' before they know the difference between virtue and vice . . . Asylums (that is, places of refuge or institutions for the afflicted) and Magdalenes are not the proper remedies for these abuses."

Both Oxford and Cambridge have colleges named after this saint, Magdalen at Oxford and Magdalene at Cambridge, and though they are spelt learnedly they are both pronounced in the common way as Maudlin. This is because, although Magdalene was early adopted as a feminine name in this country, it came to us through the French Madeleine, having already lost its *g*. The old spellings are fascinating: Maudeleyne, Mawdeleyn, Maudline, Maudlen and Madlin among others. Oddly enough, however, Maud is a different name entirely, corresponding to Matilda, hence the famous English Queen "Matilda (or Maud)", daughter of Henry I and mother of Henry III. For years she was engaged in civil war with her cousin Stephen; Matilda comes from two Germanic words *mahti* and *hildi*, meaning 'strong in battle'.

Although it was still used in the seventeenth century, Maudlin is now obsolete as a proper name, which is a pity. It seems to have been thought of after the Reformation as tainted with Popery, and was superseded by the older form Magdalen, "being no doubt taken directly from the Bible." The great Montrose married in 1629 Magdalene Carnegie, daughter of the

Earl of Southesk; but even in this form it is rarely met with nowadays. Madeleine itself we are slightly more familiar with, because of Mrs Robert Henry's cycle of books from *The Little Madeleine* onwards; it appears very seldom, however, in the births columns of *The Times* and the *Telegraph*.

In Cumberland Maudlin was corrupted even further. "The second of three Keswick fairs," once held "on the 2 August, Magdalene's Day, Old Style," was known as Morlan or Marlan Fair. The feast of Saint Mary Magdalene is, properly speaking, on 22 July, and in Devonshire it was once said that "a heavy rainfall about the middle of July shows that Saint Mary Magdalene is washing her handkerchief to go to her cousin Saint James's Fair" on 25 July.

Pleurer comme une Madeleine, says the French, means to cry abundantly. In Italy a Maddalena is *una donna coi capelli lunghi e sciolti (dalla pittura)*, a woman with long unbound hair, as in pictures of Mary Magdalene. An old Latin hymn tells how

> *Nardo Maria pistico*
> *Unxit beatos Domini*
> *Pedes, rigando lacrymis,*
> *Et detergendo crinibus.*

Mary anointed the blessed feet of the Lord with pure spikenard, washing them with her tears and wiping them with her hair— *detergendo*, from *detergere*, to wipe away or to cleanse, hence the modern detergent.

Indeed the poor lady seemed to be always crying, always playing

> a poore lamenting Mawdline's part,
> That would weepe streams of blood to be forgiven.

And this is how "mediaeval and later painters have depicted (her), with eyes red and swollen with weeping" and long, loose, dishevelled hair. Because of this *maudlin*, spelt as Magdalene was popularly pronounced, came to mean "shedding tears of penitence, like Mary Magdalene, who was taken as the type of sorrowing penitence," and then simply "weeping, tearful, lachrymose," so Dryden could speak of "their maudlin eyes".

The English mistrust easy emotion and are embarrassed by tears. Thus it was probably, as Charlotte Yonge rather pompously puts it, "from the sturdy Anglo-Saxon distaste of exhibitions of sensibility, such as were displayed in vulgar representations of her, that the contraction of her appellation came to be applied to them and especially to such affections when stimulated by intoxication." So *maudlin* was used to describe that vice universally condemned in England, sentimentality, meaning weakly, tearfully or mawkishly emotional. Donne in 1631 says, "It was a matter I might very well have left unwritten, having too much of the Maudlin humour in it."

Sometimes when a man drinks he reaches a "state of drunkenness which is characterised by the shedding of tears and effusive display of affection." He is then said to be "mawdlen drunke, when a fellow wil weepe for kindnes in the midst of his Ale and kisse you," or simply "mawdlin, weepingly drunk, as we say the Tears of the Tankard." These uses of the word are peculiarly English and do not develop in other European languages. Webster, however, recognises *maudlin* which he defines as "drunk enough to be emotionally silly."

Madeleine, of course, is also the name of a food; what Elizabeth David calls "the small, fragile, shell-shaped cakes called *madeleines* so beloved of French children." They are, incidentally, no relation at all to the English cake of the same name, "a sort of castle pudding covered with (apricot) jam and cocoanut, with a cherry on the top." How or why these small sponge buns acquired such a title is "something of a mystery".

The true madeleine is "a little cake made of flour, butter,

sugar and eggs, the same weight of each," flavoured with lemon rind and baked "in a small, grooved, deep, scallop shaped mould." It is said to have originated in the small town of Commercy in Lorraine, and to have been invented by one Madeleine Paulmier, a nineteenth-century French pastry cook, after whom it was named.

André Simon, however, has a different story. He says it was popular in Lorraine more than two hundred years ago, when it was called a *tôt-fait* because it could be made very quickly; so quickly that according to Littré, *quelques personnes l'appellent gâteau à la minute*, or minute-cakes. "In or about the year 1730," continues Simon, "the King of Poland, Stanislas Leczinski, a great gourmet and Louis XV's father-in-law, introduced the *tôt-fait* to the Versailles court, where they became fashionable. But it was only at the beginning of the nineteenth century that they were named Madeleines, by one Avice, chief pastry cook to the Prince de Talleyrand, and they have been justly popular under that name ever since." Unfortunately, however, Simon does not tell us why Avice chose this particular name.

The *OED* quotes from the *Quarterly Review* of 1922, "He is in his home in Paris, dipping a *madeleine* into a cup of tea." He, of course, is Proust, and his madeleine is surely the most famous cake in the whole of literature. For on this visit to his mother she offered him tea, and "sent out for one of those short, plump little cakes called *petites madeleines*, which look as though they had been moulded in the fluted scallop of a pilgrim's shell . . . I raised to my lips a spoonful of the tea in which I had soaked a morsel of the cake. No sooner had (it) touched my palate than a shudder ran through my whole body."

The physical sensation, familiar yet strange, excites him, brings to him an immediate reality which none the less he cannot grasp. "And suddenly the memory returns." The taste of "the little scallop-shell of pastry, so richly sensual under its severe religious folds," was "that of the little crumb of madeleine which on Sunday mornings at Cambray . . . my aunt Léonie used to give me, dipping it first in her own cup of real or lime-flower tea." At once his childhood comes flooding back to him; "the old grey house upon the street . . . rose up like the scenery of a theatre . . . and with the house the town . . . and sprang into being, town and gardens alike, from my cup of tea." The result was a masterpiece, the eight volumes of *A La Recherche du Temps Perdu*.

13

COACH AND HORSES

Un fiacre allait trottinant
Jaune avec un cocher blanc.
Derrière les stores baissés
On entendit des baisers—

so went Jean Sablon's famous song. Though this word has never found its way into English, many Englishmen during the eighteenth and nineteenth centuries were familiar with the famous Parisian *fiacres*, "a small four-wheeled carriage for hire, a hackney-coach, a French cab." But not everyone knows that they got their name from an Irish saint.

It was a certain Monsieur Sauvage who set up in business round about 1640 hiring out four-wheeled carriages or coaches by the hour. At first they were known as *carrosses à cinq sous*, since the price charged was five sous per hour. But, says Littré, the vehicles were hired out from a great house in the rue Saint-Martin in Paris, called the Hôtel *Saint-Fiacre* because an image of Saint Fiacre hung outside it, and from the Hôtel the name passed to the carriages themselves.

Somewhat oddly the *OED* maintains that Sauvage was "an inn-keeper who lived at the sign of Saint Fiacre," but there seems no authority for this beyond the fact that he occupied an *hôtel*. The Parisian *hôtels* were the town houses of the nobility; just as in London there were Somerset House and Holland House, Burlington House and Buckingham House, as it was originally called, so in Paris could be found the Hôtel de Guise, the Hôtel de Chevreuse, the Hôtel de Montmorenci and the

Hôtel de Bourgogne. Littré specifically speaks of *une grande maison*, not an inn, and confirms that *les grands, les riches, à la ville, occupent des hôtels.*

Saint Fiacre, however, was not a Frenchman but an Irish nobleman born during the seventh century and christened Fiachra or Fiachrach. Like many of his countrymen he became a monk, and left Ireland for France "in quest of closer solitude", a rather unexpected choice it would seem to us nowadays. He came to the Bishop of Meaux in the province of Brie, who promised him a place to settle and "as much land as he could turn up in a day." Like a fairy-tale character, Fiachra "instead of driving his furrow with a plough, turned the top of the soil with the point of his staff," and so got himself a sizeable parcel of land.

Here he built a cell and cultivated a garden, but though he had wanted to be alone his fame soon spread about the countryside. Many people came to see him, out of interest or curiosity, and soon he was forced to add a "hospice for travellers, where he entertained all comers," though he would not allow women to enter his church. Other buildings were added and the settlement grew, according to Butler, into "the village of Saint Fiacre in Seine et Marne." His relics are preserved at Meaux, and he became the patron saint of gardeners long before he was adopted by the cab-drivers of Paris. According to Simenon, the great Maigret's native village was Saint-Fiacre.

He was also invoked for one of the most unpleasant collection of diseases that it has fallen to the lot of any saint to be responsible for. These *maux de saint Fiacre*, so called because it was believed they could be cured by the intercession of the saint, included diarrhoea, haemorrhoids and venereal diseases, and appropriately enough warts on the knees of horses.

Not only the coach but also the coachman was called after him *un fiacre*. These gentlemen were not renowned for their polite

language; *jurer comme un fiacre* means to pronounce *beaucoup de jurements*. In England, however, we used to call a coachman, "especially one who drives at a rattling pace," a Jehu. For Jehu "the son of Jehoshaphat the son of Nimshi . . . rode in a chariot" when he went to war, and it was reported of him that "he driveth furiously". And when we swear we swear like a trooper, that is, "to indulge in very strong blasphemy or profanity," as Brewer says; though at one time it might have been a carter, a tinker or even a falconer. Earlier still comes 'to swear like a lord'; swearing, as another saying went, "came in at the head and is going out at the heels," meaning "its having once been the vice of the great, though . . . it had descended to the most low and vulgar of the people." Certainly it may have descended; it is a long time going out.

In England also from the beginning of the seventeenth century a carriage similar to the *fiacre* could be hired. This was the hackney-coach, "a four-wheeled coach drawn by two horses and seated for six persons, kept for hire." And *hackney* is a word with a very strange history.

The original hackney or *hackeneius*, as it appears in mediaeval Latin as early as 1292, was "an ambling horse or mare, especially for ladies to ride on." This use survives in the present day hack, "a horse for ordinary riding," and hacking, or riding such a horse. Skeat thinks that *hackeneius* means "belonging to Hackney in Middlesex," and no other satisfactory derivation seems to have been put forward. *Hakeneia* or *Hacanieg* as it was once spelt, has been interpreted variously as Haca's settlement, Haca's island, Haca's well-watered land or marsh, or possibly even the bend of a stream, *haca* representing not a personal name but the Old English word for a hook.

It seems likely that there was good pasture in this "well watered place" and that here horses were kept and bred on what are still known as Hackney Downs and London Fields,

K

being taken for sale to Smithfield which Stow remembered in 1603 as a great "market of horses and cattle". This "great horsemart," says Skeat, "is still connected with Hackney by Hackney Road and Mare Street," along which the horses were driven. Not everyone, however, is prepared to take Mare Street at its face value; according to *Place Names of Middlesex* it represents *mere* or *meare*, a boundary, "from its position on the parish boundary."

Similar words exist in other languages; *haquenée* in French and *hacanea* in Spanish, for instance. Before Skeat put forward this suggestion Littré recorded that *haquenée* "is said to be taken from the English *hackney*; but the English dictionaries declare that *hackney* comes from the French; it is therefore necessary to renounce this derivation." But it does seem possible that in this case at least the borrowing did go the other way and the English horses travelled across the Channel to France.

As well as being sold, "from an early date mention is found of hackneys hired out;" so early that in *Piers Plowman* Glutton drinks in the tavern with "Hikke the hakeneyman"—"one who lets horses for hire." This practice was so common that in time the word hackney itself "came often to be taken as a horse kept for hire." And when carriages began to be hired out in a similar way the same term was applied to them, so they were known as hackney carriages or coaches.

As a horse could be had for payment by the hour, so also could a man. Thus appeared the hackney writer, "one who writes for attornies or booksellers," more commonly referred to as a *hack*, "a person whose services may be hired for any kind of work required of him, especially a literary drudge, who hires himself out to do any and every kind of literary work, hence a poor writer, a mere scribbler." Such a man produces competent but unimaginative work; he is, says Partridge, "a merely industrious uncreative writer that lacks genius or talent on the one hand and genuine scholarship on the other." Johnson was comparing himself, most unfairly, with such a man when he defined a lexicographer as "a harmless drudge," and Goldsmith, "who well knew from his own experience what the life was," wrote:

> Here lies poor Ned Purdon, from misery freed,
> Who long was a bookseller's hack:
> He led such a damnable life in this world,
> I don't think he'll wish to come back.

A hackney could be had by any man who could pay, hence its use as a name for a prostitute. And something *hackneyed*, "hired or kept for hire," was subject to constant and common wear and tear. Consequently it came to be applied to words and phrases repeated *ad nauseam* and without thought, the kind of style, in fact, that a hack-writer might employ—"used so frequently and indiscriminately as to have lost its freshness and interest, made trite and commonplace, stale."

Fowler[1], on this subject of hackneyed phrases, is extremely eloquent. "There are thousands," he says, "to whose minds the cat cannot effect an entrance unaccompanied by 'harmless necessary'; nay, in the absence of the cat, 'harmless' still brings 'necessary' in its train." (Two of his own phrases here are not exactly shining new.) ". . . And the witty gentleman who equipped coincidence with her long arm has doubtless suffered . . . at seeing that arm so mercilessly overworked." He points out that for everyone there is "a moment in life" when such phrases come to him with the freshness of novelty and a delight which he amiably wishes to pass on. It does not occur to him that "though there may be one to whom (his) phrase is bright & new, it is a stale offence to the ninety & nine." While deploring the immortality achieved by the *Punch* writer whose "Advice to those

[1] Fowler, H. W. *Modern English Usage.*

about to marry" was "Don't," Fowler gives the same counsel
to a writer who finds hackneyed phrases dripping from his pen:
"What he is writing is bad stuff, or it would not need such
help; let him see to the substance of his cake instead of decorat-
ing it with sugarplums."

14

THE ALMIGHTY DOLLAR

Few people would associate what Washington Irving called in 1837 "the almighty dollar, that great object of universal devotion throughout our land," with any kind of saint. The connexion indeed is somewhat tenuous, but the story is interesting.

In what was once Bohemia and is now Czecho-Slovakia, there lay a town called Sankt Joachimsthal (later Jachymov). *Thal* is the German word for a valley; thus we speak of Neanderthal man or *Homo neanderthalis*, referring to the bones of a species of prehistoric man first found in a limestone cave in the valley of the Neander. As for Saint Joachim, Partridge says "this saint was an Italian mystic of the twelfth century." Presumably he was thinking of Joachim of Fiore or Flora, a Cistercian who spent his life in Calabria and was described by Dante as *di spirito profetico donato*, gifted with a prophetic spirit. However, though "the sanctity of his life is unquestioned," some of his views were not, and he was never canonised.

Then there is Blessed Joachim of Siena, a member of the noble Piccolomini family, who "as a child was always asking aid of his parents for those in distress, so that at last his father half in jest, bade him restrain his demands or he would reduce his family to poverty. The good man was touched but somewhat taken aback when his little son replied, 'But father, you told me yourself that what we give to the poor we give to Jesus Christ. Can we refuse him anything?' " At fourteen he became a Servite monk, and remained in Siena living a life of prayer and humility until he died in 1305. But he too is still only a *beatus*, not a saint, nor does it seem likely that his fame would have travelled to far Bohemia.

The obvious candidate is that Saint Joachim who "by pious belief" is said to have been the husband of Saint Anne or Hannah, and the father of the Blessed Virgin. Tradition says he "married at a youthful age (but) his childlessness brought public reproach, whereupon he went into the desert and prayed and fasted for forty days. An angel appeared, comforted him, and promised a child to the couple." He is, says Brewer, "generally represented as an old man carrying in a basket two turtledoves, in allusion to the offering made for the purification of his daughter." He and his wife were very popular figures in the Christian world of the Middle Ages, and it is probably from him that the valley was named.

Now Joachimsthal, as it was usually called, was "a small mining town, with mines of silver, nickel and zinc blend." Of these the silver mine, opened in 1516, was particularly famous, and from it the Counts of Schlick, who owned the land, "extracted . . . silver which they coined into ounce pieces." These pieces sometimes called *Schlickenthaler* or more commonly *Joachimsthaler*, "gained such high repute that they became a standard coin."

Almost at once this cumbersome name was shortened to *thaler* or *taler*, "a large silver coin of varying value current in the German states from the sixteenth century, especially the unit of the German monetary union (1857–73), equal to 3 marks, about 2s 11d." From German it passed into other European languages, particularly the northern countries, where it became the *daler* or *daalder* of Holland, the *rigsdaler* of Denmark and the *riksdaler* of Sweden. In France Cotgrave recorded "a curious perversion"—*jocondale*, which he defined as "a daller, a piece of money worth about 3s sterl."

Dale, of course, corresponds directly to the German *thal*, a valley, and the earliest English version of the word seems to have been *daler* or *daller*. "Of the silver coins . . . are the dalders and such, often brought over," says Harrison in 1577. But by 1618 Sylvester could pun, "For Dallers, Dolours hoardeth in my Chest," and ten years before the Fool had told King Lear, "Thou shalt have as many dolours for thy daughters as thou canst tell in a year." The spelling *dolor* appears in 1581, and by the end of the seventeenth century *dollar* had become the recognised English form.

What looks like the same word crops up in that strange nursery poem, which a certain William Howitt of Yorkshire remembered "was used to welcome late comers when he was a boy at school" about 1800:

> A diller, a dollar,
> A ten o'clock scholar,
> What makes you come so soon?
> You used to come at ten o'clock,
> And now you come at noon.

Even the Opies[1] are baffled by the first line: "Exactly what this signifies is undetermined. Crofton suggests *diller* and *dollar* are shortened forms of dilatory and dullard. Or again, diller is a Yorkshire word for a schoolboy who is dull and stupid at learning," from the old word *dill* or *dille*, sluggish, slow, dull— "Yong man is idel and old man dill" says the *Cursor Mundi* in the fourteenth century. And there is always the possibility that a dollar is a dolour, or even *dollor*, a dialect word meaning to moan, to produce a *dullor*, "a dull and moaning noise or the tune of some doleful ditty."

Though it never became an English coin, the dollar was familiar as the English name of the *peso* or piece of eight, "formerly current in Spain and the Spanish American colonies." Pieces of eight were so called because their value was that of

[1] I. and P. Opie, *The Oxford Dictionary of Nursery Rhymes.*

eight *reales*, representing in English money, says Brewer, about 1s 8d. Even allowing for considerable depreciation, a pirate ship would have to seize whole chestsful of these coins to net any appreciable sum!

Such pesos or "Philippes dolers" as they were sometimes described, circulated freely in South America and Mexico, and found their way up into the British colonies of North America. By the time of the War of Independence they had a wide currency, especially in the south, and when it became necessary to establish a common coinage for the newly formed United States it was decided to adopt the decimal system, a product of the French Revolution and so a symbol of liberty, and "resolved, that the money unit of the U.S.A. be one dollar (Spanish)."

This decision, however, was not made without discussion, and at first was nothing like as simple as it seems. H. L. Mencken in *The American Language* records how "in 1782 Gouveneur Morris proposed to the Continental Congress that the coins of the Republic be called, in ascending order, *unit, penny, bill, dollar* and *crown*." Later Morris produced the word *cent*, which he is said to have invented, "subsequently substituting it for the English penny," but *cent* is no more than the French word for a hundred, from the Latin *centum*, or a shortening of *centime*, the French coin representing *un centième du franc*, a hundredth of a franc. Morris's actual suggestion was "that the American monetary unit should be the $\frac{1}{1440}$ of a dollar, and that a coin equal to 100 of these, or $\frac{5}{72}$ of a dollar (about $3\frac{3}{4}$d English) should be made and called a cent." The reason for these somewhat extraordinary figures is that in many American colonies "accounts were kept in dollars and ninetieths, a relic of the times when the Spanish piastre . . . was worth 7s 6d (90 pence)." Thus one of the proposed units would have represented a sixteenth of a penny.

Though Gouveneur Morris's ideas were not adopted the name

of the coin was. Meanwhile Thomas Jefferson had also been trying his hand, and "after playing with such terms as *pistarine* and *piece-of-eight*, proposed *mill, cent, disme, dollar* and *eagle*, and this nomenclature was made official by the Act Establishing a Mint, approved April 2, 1792." The ninetieths had been abolished and the system was entirely decimal, a *mill* being a tenth of a cent, a *disme* ten cents, and an *eagle* "a gold coin . . . bearing an eagle on the reverse and worth ten dollars," last minted 1933.

Mencken states that "Jefferson apparently derived *disme* from the French word *dixième*, meaning a tenth, and the original pronunciation seems to have been deem." But *dime* or *disme*, from Latin *decima*, was a perfectly good French word for a tenth and more particularly for the tithes that were due to the Church. Langland knew it in the fourteenth century when he advocated the abolition of clerical property: "Take her landes, ye lordes, and let hem lyve by dymes." But in America its spelling was simplified to *dime*, soon pronounced to rhyme with *time*, and its ancient history forgotten.

As for what the *Dictionary of American English* calls "the typical or arbitrary sign of the Dollar mark $," this also seems to have been first used by Jefferson in 1784 "in the memorial which proposed the dollar as the American money-unit." Certainly it appears at first sight to have no relation to anything. "Some," says the *Dictionary*, "suppose (it) to be a monogram of, or a gerrymandered U.S." To Brewer it is "probably a modification of the figure 8 as it appeared on the old Spanish 'pieces of eight', which were of the same value as the dollar." In fact, however, it seems to have come from what Pettie in 1581 called "the noble device of Charles the fifth (of Spain), to wit, the pillars of Hercules."

These 'pillars', in other words "the rocks Calpè, now Gibraltar, and Abyla (Ceuta), on either side of the Strait of

Gibraltar," were "thought by the ancients to be the supports of the western boundary of the world and to have been set up by Hercules." Some of the old Spanish and Mexican silver pesos were "stamped on one side with what we suppose to be a re-presentation of the pillars of Hercules," and these were commonly known as pillar dollars "because they bear on the reverse the arms of Spain between two pillars." Indeed the coat of arms between two twisted pillars is still to be seen on modern Spanish coins, or was until recently.

This still seems a long way from the modern dollar-sign, but the picture becomes clearer when it is remembered that the 'pillars' were shown as upright architectural columns. These are the origin of the two parallel lines, and the S is accounted for by Webster who records another version of the pillar dollar, "having on its reverse two pillars with a ribbon about them." So though its adoption may have been "arbitrary" the dollar-sign carries a weight of tradition both Spanish and Greek far greater than most of us would ever think.

Dollar never became an English word, except to describe coins of American and other similar currencies. In the late nineteenth and twentieth centuries, however, it was re-borrowed and had some popularity as a slang term for five shillings, half a dollar being half a crown, and though monetary values are no longer comparable, these expressions are still used. Also, again through American influence, we would 'bet our bottom dollar' instead of 'putting our shirt on it' or perhaps our 'last farthing'— literally so, since like Morris's units and Jefferson's mills, these have long disappeared.

15

A PIG FOR HIS PAGE

"And what," the *Standard* in 1867 records one of our peren-
nially ignorant judges as asking, "is an 'Anthony'?" To which
comes the reply, "The littlest pig, your honour. The little pig
is always 'Anthony'." In fact it is properly known as an Antony
pig, short for a Saint Antony pig, and in common speech
usually shortened to *tantony*. A tantony was, among other
things, "the smallest pig of a litter," so called says Fuller in
1662, because "Saint Anthonie is notoriously known for the
Patron of hogs, having a pig for his Page in all pictures." Yet no
one, I think, would have been more surprised than the saint
himself at the fate of his name.

To start with we often spell it wrongly. It seems originally
to have been Antonius, the name of a Roman gens, "a word,"
says Charlotte M. Yonge, "that is not easy to trace. Some
explain it as inestimable, but the triumvir himself," the great
Mark Antony, "chose to deduce it from Antius, son of Hercules." The intrusive *h*, which has never been pronounced except
by the ignorant, may have come from the Dutch or from the
false etymology of Camden who in 1605 derived the word from
Greek *anthos*, a flower.

Certainly, as Miss Yonge so sadly complains, "modern
tongues have clipped (the sonorous) Marcus Antonius . . . By
the fifteenth century both his names had become separately
saintly and therefore mutilated; Mark in the person of the
Evangelist, Antonius in that of the great hermit of the fourth
century, the first to practise the asceticism which resulted in the
monastic system." Also, it might be added, in the person of the

thirteenth-century Franciscan, Saint Antony of Padua, Portuguese by birth and Italian by adoption, constantly invoked as the finder of things that are lost. These two made Antony a popular Christian name in all the countries of Europe.

Saint Antony the Great or Saint Antony Abbot as he is usually called, was born at Memphis in Upper Egypt in the year 251. His parents, though well-to-do, distrusted pagan scholarship like many other Christian parents since, and "kept him in ignorance of polite learning," so that he knew neither Latin nor Greek nor any language but his own. He was, however, devoutly religious and when his parents died he sold the property they left him, gave the proceeds to the poor and retired into solitude. For thirty years he lived on a mountain-side in the cruel desert of Scete, his home or cell an empty sepulchre: "The place called Scete is set in a vast desert, a day and a night from the monasteries on Nitria; and it is reached by no path, nor is the track shown by any landmarks of earth, but one journeys by the signs and courses of the stars. Water is hard to find."

Here Antony devoted himself to "the exercise of mortification and prayer, according to the import of the Greek word *askesis.*" *Askesis* means practice or training, as one would train for the Olympics; to their contemporary biographers, says Helen Waddell, "the Fathers themselves . . . are the *athletae Dei*, the athletes of God," a conception which goes back to Saint Paul: "Know ye not that they which run a race run all, but one receiveth the prize? . . . And every man that striveth for the mastery is temperate in all things . . . (So) I keep under my body, and bring it into subjection." This 'training' therefore became known as *asceticism* and those who practised it *ascetics.*

In his solitary life Antony was much troubled by the assaults of the devil, who told him he could have done much more good if he had kept his money instead of giving it away, and "harassed him night and day with gross and obscene imaginings" of beautiful naked women. This Temptation of Saint Antony "was one of the favourite subjects of mediaeval art," which always delighted in the portrayal of devils, and has appealed to writers as late as Flaubert and Ronald Duncan in *This Way to the Tomb.*

Eventually, however, Antony was persuaded out of his isolation, and is said to have founded a monastery at Faynum. This was no more than a loose community of hermits like himself, living in separate cells "sundered from one another by so wide a space that none is in sight of his neighbour, nor can any voice be heard . . . Only on the Saturday and on the Sunday do they come together to church, and there they see each other face to face as folk restored in heaven." And though he is habitually described as "the abbot Antony", an *abbas* had not yet come to mean the head of a house of monks. It was applied as a title of respect to "the senior and more reverend dwellers in the desert," rather, says Helen Waddell, like the Hebrew *Rabbi*, often translated as Master, or the French *Maître.* It was a term of affection too, for Antony was deeply loved and when, in 356, at the age of a hundred and five, "stretching out his feet a little, (he) looked joyously on death," he was also deeply mourned.

In art Saint Antony usually appears as an old and bearded man in a hermit's gown, "with a tau-shaped crutch or cross, a little bell, a pig and sometimes a book." The book is a nice piece of irony, since Antony had no learning; no doubt, says Brewer, "it has reference to the book of nature, which compensated the saint for the lack of any other reading." For when a philosopher asked him, "How dost thou content thyself, Father, who art denied the comfort of books?" he answered, "My book, philosopher, is the nature of created things, and as often as I have a mind to read the words of God, it is at my hand." Certainly he never took the trouble to learn, and in his expressed opinion that "Good sense . . . is sufficient of itself," he sounds like an Abecedarian [1] more than a thousand years before his time.

The staff he carries, "a peculiarly Egyptian T-shaped form of the cross," was popularly known as a *tantony crutch* or Saint Antony's cross. It may, says Butler, "be simply an indication of the saint's great age and abbatial authority, or it may possibly have reference to his constant use of the sign of the cross in his conflict with evil spirits." The tau-cross, also much favoured by Saint Francis, was considered to be particularly effective in tussles with the devil; it is the sign with which "in the original Greek" the redeemed in the Book of Revelation "are said to have been sealed on the forehead," and was also believed to be the mark of Cain, set on him "lest any finding him should kill him."

A crutch, once spelt *crycce* or *crucche*, "a staff for a lame or infirm person to lean upon in walking," was made for convenience sake from a T-shaped piece of wood. Since the Latin for cross is *crux*, and the Crutched Friars, the *Cruciati*, were so called because they had "a cross embroidered on their dress," it would not seem unduly rash to assume that crutch and cross are fundamentally the same word. But etymologists do not agree, saying firmly that crutch is "of unknown origin." Some relate it to Dutch *kruk*, Old French *croc*, and an Old Teutonic *kruk*, all meaning a hook or, as we would say in English, a crook, hence the bishop's crozier. Others suggest it is allied to German *kriechen*, to creep about, and compare it with cripple, one who creeps.

Antony's bell was probably also intended to chase away evil spirits, for this was the original purpose of bells, rather than to call people to church. At one time the passing bell "used to be rung when persons were *in extremis*, to scare away evil spirits which were supposed to lurk about the dying ready to pounce

[1] See p. 158.

on the soul while *passing* from the body." In the same way "consecrated bells were believed to be able to disperse storms and pestilence, drive away devils, and extinguish fire." Sometimes the bell dangles from the crutch, sometimes it is round the neck of the pig, but it is always a small one. So a *tantony* became the name for a hand-bell, "perhaps from a swine-herd's use of one for calling his charges to their meal," or more particularly a small church bell. In a Northamptonshire Glossary *Tantony* is defined as "the small bell over the church porch or between the chancel and the nave"; it was also said to be "the name given to a bell which is rung at the entrance gate of the grounds at Kimbolton Castle to give notice of the arrival of visitors."

But it is for his pig that Saint Antony is perhaps best known. "Saint Antony the hermit," says Grose, uncharacteristically ill-informed, "was a swineherd, and is always represented with a swine's bell and a pig." Certainly he was adopted as the patron of swineherds, as also of "domestic animals and farm stock, of butchers and of brush-makers," who used hog's bristles. Yet he was never a swineherd in his life, nor had he any connexion with pigs. The animal is a symbol of "the unclean demon" whose temptations he resisted; one of the Gadarene swine into which entered the devils whose name was Legion, "for we are many." It was not until the Middle Ages, when such symbolism began to lose its hold, that "the pig placed at his feet . . . was by popular ignorance supposed to be an animal dedicated to him."

Meanwhile Antony had acquired a secondary reputation, this time as a healer. In later pictures he is often shown surrounded by flames, "which are typical of the disease, Saint Antony's Fire, against which the saint was specially invoked." This disease, "called also the 'burning sickness', 'hell fire' or 'sacred fire'," in German *Antonsfeuer* and in French *feu saint Antoine*, has been identified with erysipelas, a Greek word meaning a reddening, *erythos*, of the *pella*, skin, and ironically christened in Welsh *y fendigaid*, the blessed. It was accompanied by fever, red rash and a burning sensation of the skin, and in the days of over-crowded and insanitary hospitals spread 'like wildfire'. Flames were an apt symbol.

Nowadays, however, it seems likely that Saint Antony's Fire was not originally erysipelas but "a far more virulent and contagious disorder caused probably by the consumption of flour made from grain damaged by ergot." This *ergot* or *argot*, a French word meaning, according to Cotgrave, "the Spurre of a Cocke, the heel or talon of a Hog," is used to describe a disease of rye and other cereals. It is caused by a fungus *Claviceps purpurea*, which distorts the grain so that it becomes "in colour dark violet, and in form resembling a cock's spur, hence the name."

Throughout Europe the poorer people lived on rye bread, and could not afford to throw away diseased crops. But the fungus was highly toxic, and afflicted those who ate bread made from infected grain with ergot poisoning. They developed muscular spasms, "numbness, tingling and severe pains . . . in the ex-tremities," the gradual production of gangrene caused by the contraction of tiny blood vessels, and finally a tendency for "parts like the fingers, toes and tips of the ears" to mortify and become black, "as though consumed by internal fire," then to shrivel and drop off. As late as the nineteenth century a hospital in Vienna used to show "withered and blackened limbs, relics of the afflicted." Several terrible epidemics of this mysterious scourge occurred in France and Germany during the Middle Ages, and it was after one such outbreak in 1089, "when many were said to have been cured after making intercession to him," that the disease became widely known as Saint Antony's Fire.

About this time a certain Gaston de Dauphiné begged the help of the saint on behalf of his son who was stricken with the

feu saint Antoine. The boy recovered, and in gratitude his father founded a religious congregation, the Hospital Brothers of Saint Antony, to care for all those suffering from this disease and for the "hordes of crippled vagrants roaming Europe" who had recovered but as a result of the illness lost the use of one or more of their limbs. A similar order of Canons Regular of Saint Antony seems also to have been founded almost simultaneously in Vienna by "a prior named Antony." They wore on their habits, says Littré, "the figure of a T: it represents a crutch for walking"—in this case singularly apt. Moreover the doors of of their hospitals were "always painted red or flame coloured," and often they displayed pictures of Saint Antony with his hog, "while a maimed sufferer on a crutch holds up an arm from which bursts flames."

This order established itself in England. Stow describes how on the north side of what he calls "three needle street . . . you come to the hospital of S. Anthonie, sometime a Cell to saint Anthonies of Vienna." This land, he says, was granted to them by Henry III, who gave them "a place amongst the Iewes, which was sometime their Sinagogue." Here a hospital was built which "was called saint Anthonies in London . . . in the parish of saint Bennet Finke, for a Master, two Priests, one Schoolmaster and 12 poore men." It also had "a large free school" and "Almes houses of hard stone and timber." Other similar houses were opened in different parts of England; that there was one in York is shown by a will dated 1515 in which the testator bequeaths "to every Tanten man ther dwellyng, iiijd, to pray for my sowll." A *Tanten* or *Tanton man* was "an inmate of a hospital or the like dedicated to Saint Anthony," one of Stow's "poore men."

It is now that we begin to hear of the pig again. This creature which "in its origin denoted the devil" had by the twelfth century "acquired a new significance," says Butler, "owing to

L

the popularity of the Hospital Brothers of Saint Antony, founded at Clermont in 1096. Their works of charity endeared them to the people, and they obtained in many places the privilege of feeding their swine gratuitously upon the acorns and beech mast in the woods. For this purpose a bell was attached to the neck of one or more sows in a herd of pigs, or probably their custodians announced their coming by ringing a bell. In any case it seems that the bell became associated with the members of the order, and in that way developed into an attribute of their eponymous patron." Since these animals "lived at free quarters" and did very well for themselves, Miss Yonge quotes "as fat as a Tantony pig" as becoming a proverb. But I have not found this saying anywhere else.

In England the pigs seem to have roamed the towns rather than the fields and woods. "Rene thou not fro hous to house lyke a nantyny gryce,[1]" adjured a writer as early as 1460. And Grose, who gives "to follow like a tantony pig" as meaning "to follow close at one's heels," explains it thus: "Some derive this saying from a privilege enjoyed by the friars of certain convents in England and France (sons of Saint Antony) whose swine were permitted to feed in the streets. These same would follow anyone having greens or other provisions, till they obtained some of them; and it was in those days considered an act of charity to feed them."

Stow, however, in his *Survey of London*, gives from his own experience a rather different story. "And amongst other things observed in my youth, I remember that the Officers charged with the oversight of the Markets in this Citie, did divers times take from the Market people pigs sterved or otherwise unholsome for man's sustenance, these they slit in the ears; one of the Proctors for saint Anthonies tyed a bell about the necke, and let it feed on the Dunguehils, no man would hurt or

[1] young pig.

take them up, but if any gave to them bread, or other feeding, such would they know, watch for and dayly follow, whining till they had some what given them: whereupon was raysed a proverbe, such a one will follow such a one, and whine as it were an Anthonie pig: but if such a pig grew to be fat, and came to good liking (as oft times they did), then the Proctor would take him up to the use of the Hospitall."

So a *tantony* came to mean a man who fawns and whines. "Some," says Gauden in 1659, "are such Cossets and Tantanies that they congratulate their Oppressors and flatter their Destroyers." And Stow's "proverbe" seems to have had a certain amount of currency during the seventeenth and eighteenth centuries. Thus Chapman in 1606 writes, somewhat oddly, "I have followed you up and down like a Tantalus pig." And in Swift's *Polite Conversation* Lady A. remarks, "She made me follow her last Week through the Shops like a Tantiny Pig," a complaint which many a husband must have echoed since. Tantony or tantany could also become a verb: "Do not follow and tantany us, Mr Ramble," exclaims an indignant mamma in 1675, "for thou shalt never have my daughter." It seems a pity such an expressive and pleasant sounding word should have fallen out of favour.

Chambers's Cyclopaedia in 1753 reported that "in several places they (Romanists) keep at common charges a hog, denominated Saint Anthony's hog." But this variant of the 'town bull' is probably no more than a misconception. Nor does any of this history, except perhaps Stowe's recollections of "pigs sterved or otherwise unholsome," tie in with Partridge's quotation from a Hertfordshire Dialect Glossary that "we call a poor starved creature a Tantony pig." But the *OED* maintains that as Saint Antony was the patron of swineherds, "one of each litter was usually vowed" to him; hence Antony or tantony is "the smallest pig of the litter". This might seem to imply that if you are required to give something away you choose the worst and the weakest.

Yet tantony, like *cosset*, the name for "a pet lamb brought up in the house," was surely a term of affection, for the most care has to be given to those least likely to survive, and "the smallest pig of a litter," says Brewer, getting his facts slightly wrong, "according to the old proverb, will follow its owner anywhere" in exactly the same way as Mary's little lamb, which was obviously a cosset. Tantony might have become, as Ivor Brown suggests, "a synonym for darling" if its earlier history had not associated it with flattery, whining and greed.

16

TITTLE EST AMEN

Criss-cross sounds a simple word; a mere reduplication like tip-top, zig-zag, ding-dong. Its meaning seems equally obvious— "in cross lines, crosswise, at cross purposes, work with a criss-cross pattern." But these uses do not occur until the nineteenth century, one of the earliest being from Keats who announced his intention "to criss-cross the letter" he was writing—that is to fill the page then turn it round and continue writing across and at right angles to the lines already completed. This was done to save postage, charged at so much a sheet.

By this time the origin of criss-cross had already been forgotten. That it was not a simple jingle can be seen from the alternative spelling *croscrist*. Originally, of course, it was Christ-cross or Christ's cross, the pronunciation being slurred as it is in Christmas.

Christ-cross or criss-cross was "the figure or mark of a cross in general," sometimes upright, sometimes diagonal, what we would call an X. This figure, being a symbol of Christianity and also comparatively easy even for an uneducated person to recognise and draw, has been accepted for centuries as the signature of those unable to sign their name, and commonly known as "John Doe, his mark." John Doe, of course, is merely a man of straw, "an imaginary person put forward for some reason," like the A. N. Other who plays in cricket matches or the Walter Plinge who appears on theatre programmes. As late as 1846 Brockett was defining *Cris-cross* as "the mark of signature of those who cannot write."

It is probably this, combined with the use of *x* to denote an

153

'unknown quantity', which accounts for our habit of almost unconsciously drawing a cross on a map or a postcard—X marks the spot. The Christ-cross also stood in the place of twelve o'clock on the sundial. But what brought it into common everyday speech was the invariable practice of placing it at the beginning of the alphabet on hornbooks from which for centuries English children learned their letters. As a reformer, who violently disapproved of even the least whiff of Popery, wrote in 1640, "the beginning of learning is the letters, and the beginning of the letters is . . . that most profane, superstitious and Anti-christian letter which they call Chriss-crosse." In spite of his disapproval the anti-christian letter remained until hornbooks disappeared,

Nor were they in fact books at all. They consisted of one sheet, at first of vellum and later of paper, on which was written or printed "the alphabet, often with the addition of the ten digits, some elements of spelling and the Lord's Prayer," or before the Reformation the Paternoster. This sheet was protected from general wear and tear by a thin covering of horn, for a long time one of the very few transparent materials known and also used for window panes and in horn-lanterns to protect the naked flame from the wind. Finally the whole was slotted into a wooden, usually oaken frame, shaped roughly like a table-tennis bat and a little larger. A cord was attached to the handle and when not in use the hornbook hung at the child's belt or girdle. The back of the hornbook, says Brewer, "was often ornamented with a rude sketch of Saint George and the Dragon," and he quotes the eighteenth-century poet Thomas Tickell, who went so far as to compose an ode to his Horn Book:

Thee will I sing, in comely wainscot bound—

Wainscot, incidentally was in the fourteenth century "superior oak boarding imported from the Continent," and later any wooden panelling; it represents a German *wagenshot*, presumably from *wagen*, meaning a waggon or wain, and *schot*, some kind of boarding or planking.

> Thee will I sing, in comely wainscot bound,
> And golden verge inclosing thee around:
> The faithful horn before, from age to age
> Preserving thy invulnerable page;
> Behind, thy patron saint in armour shines,
> With sword and lance to guard the sacred lines.

The "sacred lines", according to the *Encyclopaedia Britannica*, consisted of "first a large cross—the criss-cross—from which the hornbook was called the Christ cross row or Criss cross row. The alphabet in large and small letters followed. The vowels formed a line and their combinations with the consonants were given in tabular form. The usual exorcism—'in the name of the Father and of the Sonne and of the Holy Ghost, Amen'— followed, then the Lord's prayer, the whole concluding with the Roman numerals."

The Pilgrim Fathers and other American settlers took the hornbook with them, and one at least surviving from colonial times is marked with a stately heading certifying that it is "The ABC set forthe by the Kynges Majestie and his Clergy, and commaunded to be taught throughout all his Realme. All other utterly set apart, as the Teachers thereof tender his Graces Favour." It would scarcely seem that the alphabet could be a matter for political and theological dispute, but basic learning in those days was incomplete without simple prayers and religious symbols, and a people who once described the cross as "profane, superstitious and Anti-christian" could most certainly "find quarrel in a straw".

Others, anxious to help the spread of literacy, left money in their wills "for the buyeing and provideing of horne bookes and primers to be given to poore children." Less seriously Prior in 1717 records what must be one of the earliest examples of the Play Way in education:

> To Master John the English maid
> A hornbook gives of gingerbread,
> And that the child may learn the better,
> As he can read, he eats the letter.

It is to be hoped he wasn't too slow in learning, or his gingerbread primer would have got rather stale.

"Hornbooks," says Brewer, "were in use in elementary schools for the poor when books were scarce and expensive," and survived considerably longer than that. The *OED* quotes "a large wholesale dealer in school requisites" who recollected that "the last order he received for Horn-books came from the country, about the year 1799. From that time the demand wholly ceased . . . In the course of sixty years, he and his predecessors in business had executed orders for several millions of Horn-books." And as late as 1863 Kingsley wrote in *The Water-Babies* of a dame-school kept by an old woman "in her red petticoat and short dimity bedgown, and clean white cap . . . and opposite her sat, on two benches, twelve or fourteen neat, rosy, chubby little children, learning their Chris-cross-row; and gabble enough they made about it."

Cotgrave in 1611 translated *La croix de par Dieu* as "the Christs-cross-row, or the hornebook wherein a child learnes it." More usually the Chriss-cross-row was the alphabet itself. So a writer in 1602 recorded his slow academic progress thus: "I was five year learning cris-crosse from great A"—or as we should call it, capital A—"and five yeere longer in coming to F," which certainly puts him among the backward readers. Sterne's *Tristram Shandy* was much more advanced, having spent only "four years travelling from Crist-cross-row to Malachi," the Old Testament being the reading book of the highest class and Malachi being the last of the Minor Prophets.

As for the gentleman who admitted as early as 1401, "I know not an A from the Wyndemylne, ne a B from a bole foot," he was accusing himself of being totally illiterate. And the caustic dismissal of a stupid person as someone who doesn't know a B—or as it was often written later, through misunderstanding, a bee—from a bull's foot, is still at least partially current. There seems no particular reason for the choice of a bull's foot; at one time the phrase was more commonly 'not to know a B from a battledore'.

Now the game of battledore and shuttlecock, "in which the shuttlecock is hit with the battledore backwards and forwards between two players, or by one player into the air, as many times as possible without dropping it," seems to have been popular in England as an indoor game, a "winter recreation" along with "cardes and bailliards", at least from the sixteenth century. "The Shuttel-Cocke," it was said, "with the Batteldoore is a pretty house-exercise." But the battledore, a kind of small light racquet, either strung or solid, got its name from its shape and originally was a much more utilitarian instrument.

"Batyldoure," says one of the earliest definitions, "a wasshynge betylle," that is a beetle or wooden bat "for beating clothes while being washed." The etymology, according to the experts, is "not at all certain," but is probably connected with Spanish *batir*, to beat, and more directly with the Provençal *batedor*, a beater. The shape of this beater or bat was also the shape of the hornbook; it is easy to imagine unruly children using them as such in their games. Certainly the hornbooks became known as battledores, especially the later, rather less clumsy versions, made often of stiff paper and dispensing with the wooden frame. In 1877 Peacock decribed a "Battledoor" as "a piece of cardboard on which was printed the ABC, the Lord's Prayer and a few short syllables, employed as a substitute for the hornbook. They were in use . . . in dames' schools, thirty years ago." Almost certainly this is what Kingsley's chubby children were learning from.

To test a child's knowledge the teacher would point to a letter and expect him to repeat its name. If he 'did not know a B from a battledore' then he had learnt nothing and might be considered "to be quite illiterate, not even to know (his) letters." The comparable proverb 'to say B to a battledore' meant "to open one's mouth to speak"; someone who couldn't say B to a battledore was either stupid or else timid, shy, unassertive. The timidity was emphasised when B was written Bo and interpreted as Boh or Boo, "an exclamation intended to surprise or frighten." Saying Bo to a goose once had the same meaning; now we think of someone who 'daren't say Boo to a goose' as lacking in self-confidence and courage.

The child learning his letters was sometimes known as a battledore boy or as an abecedarian, a term at one time in common use in the United States. The same word could also describe the man who taught him; "an Abecedarie or teacher of petties," as Minsheu defined it in 1623. And it was even applied in the sixteenth century to a member of an Anabaptist sect (Anabaptists being those who "did not believe in infant baptism and hence were baptized over again, *ana*, on coming to years of discretion") that "regarded the teaching of the Holy Spirit . . . as sufficient for every purpose in life, and hence despised all learning of every kind, except so much of the ABC as was necessary to enable them to read the Scriptures."

Spelt sometimes abecedarius, it stands also for a kind of

acrostic poem "in which the lines or stanzas begin with the letters of the alphabet in regular order." Such is Chaucer's *A.B.C.*, a hymn to the Virgin which he calls *carmen secundem ordinem literarum Alphabeti*, or the 119th Psalm, where "the first eight verses . . . in the original begin with *Aleph*, which is the name of the first letter of the Hebrew alphabet. The second eight verses begin with *Beth*, the name of the second letter . . . and so on to the end of the whole alphabet, in all twenty-two letters, each letter having eight verses." Bishop Challoner could, however, find no reason for this display of virtuosity; he continues his note by remarking, with more modesty than the Anabaptists, that "this order is variously expounded by the holy fathers; which shews the difficulty of understanding the holy scriptures."

All these learned words with their various spellings are of course elaborations of the letters ABC or ABCD. Written out, these appear in a number of strange forms—abece, abeesee, absee, apsie, even apecy—commonly used from the thirteenth century to describe the English alphabet. When the Greek word *alphabetos*, or rather its Latin form *alphabetum*, began to appear at the end of the sixteenth century it was properly employed only to describe "the set of letters used in writing the Greek language". Thus Cotgrave in 1611 writes pedantically of "the French *abece*, for Alphabet I will not call it, according to the vulgar error, that word being peculiar only to the Greek tongue." He was, however, like all linguistic purists in all centuries, fighting a losing battle.

Alphabet, now meaning generally "any set of characters representing the simple sounds used in a language or in speech," is simply "the first two Greek letters (*alpha*, *beta*) taken as a name for the whole." According to Skeat these letters are "from Phoenician names represented by Hebrew *aleph*, an ox, also the name of the first letter of the Hebrew alphabet; and *beth*, a house, also the name of the second letter of the same." To Eusebius, however, "*Alph* translated into the Greek language could mean 'learning'", and some say the symbol for *beth* represents the door of a house, thus the alphabet was regarded quite literally as the gateway to learning. According to Brewer it is "the only word of more than one syllable compounded solely of the names of letters." And even this piece of singularly useless information can at least be questioned.

For the abece or absey is also another name for the hornbook or for "a spelling book or primer teaching the alphabet and first elements of reading":

> Quan a chyld to scole xal set be,
> A bok hym is browt, naylyd on a brede of tre,[1]
> That men callyt an abece.

The ABC or absey-book seems also to have contained "a few rudimentary lessons, often set in catechism form." Thus the Bastard in *King John*, carrying on an imaginary conversation, says

> . . . that is question now;
> And then comes answer, like an absey-book.

Nowadays, of course, if a man asked for an ABC he would most probably expect to get the "ABC Rail Guide, showing at a glance how and when to travel from London to the Principal Railway Stations in Great Britain and return . . . with other useful information."

Since monks were the first teachers the recitation of the alphabet began not only with a cross, but with a prayer, the usual formula being "Christ's cross me speed". "How long agoo learned ye Christ Cross me spede?" cried Lydgate in

---

[1] piece of wood.

1420; "Have ye no more lernyd of youre a,b,c?" And Morley in 1597 gives in full one of the many versions in which children repeated their letters:

"Christes crosse be my speede, in all vertue to proceede.
A, b, c, d, e, f, g, h, i, k, l, m, n, o, p, q, r, s, & t, double w, v, x with y, ezod,
& per se, con per se, tittle tittle est Amen.
When you have done, begin againe, begin againe."

Apart from its unexpected echoes of *Michael Finnegan*, the first point of interest is that there are only twenty-four letters, not twenty-six. At least until the seventeenth century *i* and *j* were interchangeable, and so were *u* and *v*, so only one is listed in each case. Also, somewhat surprisingly, *w* comes before and not after *v*. Although this letter is called a double-u, it is actually written in capitals as a double V—VV—since "V was formerly the symbol of U as well as V"—another example of the delightful illogicality of the English language.

Then there is ezod, an unusual spelling of the letter we commonly call *zed*. This letter, perhaps the least used of the twenty-six, has had by far the widest variety of names, all of which derive ultimately from the Greek *zeta*, which comes seventh in the Greek alphabet, *omega* being the last. The American *zee*, which is its usual description in the United States, "seems to have had some early currency in English," but it died out along with all the other rather bizarre-looking spellings—zad, zard, izzard, izzet, uzzard, uzzit, ezod.

Izzard, of which most of the others are variants, was perhaps the most widely used. Johnson in 1755 gives "Zed, more commonly izzard or uzzard", and goes on to suggest a most ingenious derivation—"that is *s hard*". Unfortunately he either ignored or had never heard of the existence of a Provençal form *izeto*, to which all these names are probably related.

M

Izzard, also Issett, Issitt and the like, occurs as a surname, but this, say etymologists, has no connexion with the letter *z*. It is a corruption of the feminine name Iseult or Isolde, much favoured in the Middle Ages because of the romantic Arthurian legend of Tristram and Iseult, and seems to have been derived from the German *is hild*, ice-battle, or even *is vald*, ice-rule, strange titles for any woman, especially the heroine of one of the timeless love stories of the world. In English the name was usually written Isot or Izot, latinised as Isota, which could quite easily become confused with *izzet* or *ezod*, and so with *izzard* itself.

In *King Lear* Kent in a fury addresses Goneril's steward Oswald as "Thou whoreson zed! Thou unnecessary letter!" As a term of abuse, however, it never attained any popularity. To Grose *zad* meant "crooked like the letter *z*. He is a mere *zad*, or perhaps zed; a description of a very crooked or deformed person." And then there was Zedland, the "great part of the west country", that is "the counties of Devonshire, Dorsetshire, and Somersetshire," where "the letter Z is substituted for S; as zee for see, zun for sun, etc, etc."

Some letters in English are also words—A, for instance, and O and I. Children reciting their Criss-cross-row were taught in these cases to say 'A per se A; I per se I', and so on; that is, "A by itself makes the word A", and because of this the letter itself was also sometimes known as A-per-se. Standing as it does at the beginning of the alphabet, this soon became a natural phrase to describe "the first, chief, most excellent, most distinguished or unique person or thing, one who is *facile princeps*, or in the modern phrase A1." A1 is perhaps not so modern a phrase for 'top of the pops' as when the *OED* was compiled; nothing changes so quickly as slang, yet it lingers with us still.

A-per-se, however, was not slang and the poets, especially in

Scotland, always famed for its education, delighted to use it. Dunbar, invoking London as

> Gemme of all joy, jasper of jocunditie,
> Most myghty carbuncle of vertue and valour,

begins his poem

> London, thou art of townes *A per se.*

and in the *Gude and Godlie Ballates* appearing in 1578 we find

> Christ Jesus is ane A per C,
> And peirless Prince of all mercy.

At the end of the hornbook came &, the sign for *and*, now known as the *ampersand*, a word peculiar to English. This symbol, says Brewer, "is an adaptation of the written *et* (Latin and), the transformation of which can be traced if we look at the italic ampersand *&*, where the *e* and the cross of the *t* are clearly recognisable." This used to be known, when a classical education was the rule, as the Tironian sign, after Marcus Tullius Tiro, the freedman and amanuensis of Cicero. Taking down his master's fluent and eloquent dictation, he is said to have invented or introduced a system of shorthand, called the *notae Tironianae* or Tironian notes, including the contraction *&* for *et*.

But our word ampersand once again goes right back to the child learning his letters. It is "a corruption of 'and per se and', the old way of spelling and naming the character &, that is, and by itself = and, and is found in various forms in almost all the dialect Glossaries." Some of these forms are rather charming— ampassy-and, ampussy-and, ampusand, and even ampassy or ampussy *tout court*, sounding like characters from Ian Fleming. The sign itself looks rather like a rough drawing of a cat, and it would be tempting to associate it with the strange word puss or pussy, if *puss* hadn't once meant a hare and if there wasn't a corresponding *pūs* or *pūskatte* in Low German and *poes* in Dutch.

America occasionally substituted an izzard or a zee for the *s*, amperzand. Webster, asserting pontifically that the ampersand was not a letter called forth in 1845 a burst of indignation: "Webster, moreover, advertises us that & is no letter; the goal of every breathless, whip-fearing abecedarian's valorous strife, the high-sounding Amperzand, no letter!"

The alphabet very properly concludes with Amen, but what of the "tittle tittle est"? *Tittle* here means a point, a dot, a punctuation mark or full stop. Three dots in an ascending line (.·˙) were usually put at the end of the letters on hornbooks, and after them came *Est Amen*. Even this was part of the child's religious education. "In old time," explained a writer in 1630, "they used three prickes at the latter end of the Cross row . . . which they caused children to call tittle, tittle, tittle; signifying that as there were three prickes and those three made but one stop, even so there were three Persons and yet but one God." As with the beginning, so with the end; the familiar phrase 'tittle est Amen' came to be used for the finish or the conclusion. "This is the Tittle est amen of it," wrote Nashe in 1594.

Tittle originally seems to have come to us from Wyclif. In the King James Bible Jesus says, "Till heaven and earth pass, one jot or one tittle shall in no wise pass from the law until all be fulfilled." The Vulgate has *iota unum, aut unus apex non praeteribit a lege, donec omnia fiant*, and the Greek words corresponding to *iota* and *apex* are *iota* and *keraia*. Wyclif's translation is "oon i or titil" and this Tyndale later adapted to "one iott or one tytle", so giving us the phrase 'no jot or tittle' which can sometimes still be heard.

Skeat rather clouds the issue by defining jot by tittle and tittle by jot. But though they have both come to mean "the very least or a very little part of something, a minute amount, a whit," as when Portia says to Shylock, "This bond doth give thee here no jot of blood," there is a difference. *Iota* is, of course, the letter *i*, "the smallest letter in the Greek alphabet," and is sometimes used in English in its original form, which makes it another "word of more than one syllable compounded solely of the names of letters." Because of the interchangeable *i* and *j* it was sometimes written *jota*, then the *a* was changed to an *e*, giving *iote* or *jote*, both pronounced as monosyllables. So we get Tyndale's *iott* and finally jot.

Tittle has a rather more complicated history. The Greek *keraia* meant literally a little horn, and thus "any minute point or part of a letter". Saint Jerome translated *keraia* by *apex*, a point or a tip, which had the same meaning in classical Latin; it also applied by extension to "any stroke or tick with the pen," such as an accent or a line drawn over a vowel to indicate that it was long. Shakespeare's Moth quotes what is clearly a schoolboys' joke: "What is a, b, spelt backward, with the horn on his head?" To which the answer is, "Ba! most silly sheep with a horn."

The Latin *titulus*, which by another route became our word title and was first used in English for the inscription affixed by Pilate to the cross, also meant for the Latin grammarians "a small stroke or point in writing", the Spanish *tilde*. Wyclif, therefore, substituted *titulus* for *apex* and translated it as titil; the spelling tittle is later, not appearing till the seventeenth century. Even the 1611 Bible has title, though "modern printers have altered it."

A tittle, then could be "any small mark distinguishing one letter from another, like the stroke of a *t*," or the dot over an *i*. This dot was "not originally part of the letter, but was introduced about the eleventh century" by the scribes and copyists "as a diacritic (from Greek *dia crinein*, to separate) in cases where two *i*'s came together (e.g. *filii*) to distinguish between these and *u*." Thus to dot one's *i*'s and to cross one's *t*'s is to make oneself perfectly plain, to "perfect some piece of work by putting the last finishing touches to it".

From the dot on an *i* to a punctuation mark, especially a full point, or even to the pip on a dice, is an easy transition. But it can be said that a jot is the letter *i* and a tittle is the dot above it. Mrs Mary Delany, a court lady and friend of Swift, writing in 1783 recorded the following conversation: "Ye person said, 'ye Dk (of Marlborough) puts no tittles upon the i's.' 'O,' says ye Prince (Eugene), 'it saves his Grace's ink.' "

But a tittlebat has nothing to do with a tittle or even a horn-book; it is a child's name for a stickleback, a wilful or ignorant mispronunciation, though it may have been influenced by memories of 'tittle tittle est'. Keats in his charming children's poem *A Song about Myself*, seems to have been the first writer to use it, but it must have been current long before. He tells of "a naughty boy" who would get up early and go to the brook

> And bring home
> Miller's thumb
> Tittlebat,
> Not over fat.

Tittlebat was said in 1887 to be "a vulgar London variant" of stickleback, so this is probably one of Keats' cockneyisms.

Fishing for the same fish, perhaps in the same waters, there was Samuel Pickwick, Esq, "the man who had traced to their source the mighty ponds of Hampstead, and agitated the scientific world with his Theory of Tittlebats." It sounds as if Dickens is here gently mocking the expeditions to trace the sources of the Nile and the Theory of Evolution. Yet *Pickwick Papers* appeared in 1837; the first Egyptian Nile Expedition set out in 1839 and Darwin did not make public his theory until 1858.

Now, alas, tittlebats are seldom, if ever, heard of. Like most other words in this chapter, they are fast becoming extinct. And though I can't keep them alive I am glad to record that they lived before they finally reach their 'tittle est amen'.

BIBLIOGRAPHY

The following are the books to whose authors I am most indebted:

Brewer, E. Cobham *Dictionary of Phrase and Fable.* Cassell and Co., London. N.D.

Butler's Lives of the Saints (revised by H. Thurston, S. J., and Donald Attwater). Burns and Oates, London. 1956.

Grose, F. (ed. E. Partridge) *A Classical Dictionary of the Vulgar Tongue.* Routledge and Kegan Paul, London. 1963.

Littré, E. *Dictionnaire de la Langue Française.* Gallimard/Hachette. 1964 (revised edition).

Onions, C. T. *The Oxford Dictionary of English Etymology.* Oxford University Press. 1966.

Partridge, E. *A Dictionary of the Underworld.* Routledge and Kegan Paul, London. 1949.

Partridge, E. *Origins.* Routledge and Kegan Paul, London. 1958.

Partridge, E. *A Dictionary of Slang and Unconventional English.* Routledge and Kegan Paul, London. 1961.

Reaney, P. H. *A Dictionary of British Surnames.* Routledge and Kegan Paul, London. 1958.

Skeat, W. W. *An Etymological Dictionary of the English Language.* Oxford University Press. 1963 (revised edition).

Withycombe, E. G. *The Oxford Dictionary of English Christian Names.* Oxford University Press. 1950.

Wright, A. R. *British Calendar Customs.* Folk-lore Society, London. 1936.

Yonge, C. M.) *History of Christian Names.* Parker, Son and Bourne, London. 1863.

Webster's Third New International Dictionary of the English Language. G. and C. Merriam, Mass., U.S.A. 1961.

And of course:

A New English Dictionary on Historical Principles. Oxford University Press. (Cited as *OED*.)

INDEX OF WORDS

171

Coventry, send to, 73–74
Criss-cross, 153–155
Criss-cross-row, 155–157
Crutch, 146
Cursitor, 59

Dampier, 96–97
Dime, 141
Dollar, 137–142
Dollar, pillar, 142
Dollar sign, 141–142
Dower, 73
Drawers, 1

Erysipelas, 147
Expedite, 82
Expeditus, St, 81–82

Farce (cookery), 13–14
    (liturgical), 15–16
    (mockery), 19–20
    (theatrical), 16–19
Fiacre, 131–133
Forcemeat, 13–14
Friar (printing), 44

Genius, 25
Gibberish, 58–59

Hack, 134–135
Hackney, 133–135
Hackneyed, 135–136
Handicap, 91–92

Harlequin, 7
Harlot, 54–55
Hornbook, 154–156
Horseplay, 19
Hose, 1–3

Impede, 82
Izzard (letter Z), 161
    (name), 162

Jargon, 62
Jehu, 133
Jot, 164–166

Kapelle, 42
Kapellmeister, 42

Lazar, 70–72
Lazaretto, 72
Leprous, 71
Liberata, St, 79
Livery, 80–81
Lizard, The, 71–72
Lupercalia, 85–86

Madeleine (cake), 128–130
Madelonettes, 125
Magdalene (hospital), 125–126
    (name), 124, 126
    (prostitute), 125
Malinger, 60, 66
Maltalent, 21